Northern Frights

Northern Frights

A Supernatural Ecology of the Wisconsin Headwaters

Dennis Boyer

Illustrations by Owen Coyle

PRAIRIE OAK PRESS
Madison, Wisconsin

First edition, first printing
Copyright © 1998 by Dennis Boyer

Prairie Oak Press
821 Prospect Place
Madison, Wisconsin 53703

Typeset by Quick Quality Press, Madison, Wisconsin
Printed in the United States of America
by BookCrafters, Chelsea, Michigan

Library of Congress Cataloging-in-Publication Data

Boyer, Dennis.
   Northern frights: a supernatural ecology of the Wisconsin head-waters / Dennis Boyer; illustrations by Owen Coyle. -- 1st ed.
      p.   cm.
   Includes index.
   ISBN 1–879483–53–X
   1. Legends—Wisconsin. 2. Tales—Wisconsin. 3.—Ghosts—Wisconsin. 4. Indians of North America—Wisconsin—Folklore.
I. Title.
GR110.W5B695 1998
398.2'09775—dc21
                                                98-8584
                                                 CIP

In Memory of
Tom Saunders
and
Sparky Waukau

Contents

Part I Lake Superior Slope

Part II Lake and Loon Country

Part III Heart of the North

Part IV Abandoned Fields and Jack Pine Shacks

Part V Portage to the South

Acknowledgments

To those who shaped my view of Wisconsin's Northwoods:

Paul Gilk, Jim & Pam Wise, Frank Koehn, Walt Bresette, Julie Wurl-Koth, Randy Rossing, Al Gedicks, Nick Hockings, Jim Chizek, Judy Borke, Joel McOlash, Nettie Kingsley, Jeff Peterson, Justin Isherwood, Rick Whaley, Ellen Smith, Lisa Johnson, Evelyn Churchill, Michael Prusak, Bob Kasper, Jeannine Wahlquist, Bill Hurrle, Herb Buettner, Paul DeMain, Tom Ourada, Jim Schlender, Frank Boyle, Tom Thornton, Terry Musser, Mick Sagrillo, Jim Holperin, and the customers at Witz End in Stevens Point and Molly's Grill in Black River Falls. Thanks!

To those who assisted with helping me presume to understand some of the tales I heard:

Anne Stevens, Roxie Owens, Dick Arneson, Nick Meiers, Archie Mosay, Sheri Matheson, Bobby Bullet St. Germaine, Gary Burkum, Glenn Little Deer, Michael Norman, Bill Steigerwaldt, Eddie Benton-Banai, Laurie Melrood, Blake Gentry, Miriam Brown, Jeannette Feldballe, Russ Moody, Dan Yoder, Esther Burkholder, Delores Chilsen Mielke, the staff of the Madeline Island Museum, the Oneida Nation, the Red Cliff Chippewa, the Stockbridge-Munsee, and the Ho Chunk Historic Preservation Office, Allen Ruff, the Mennonite Ecology Group, the Sinsinawa Eco-spirituality Group, and the Wisconsin Greens. Blessings upon you!

To the readers, bookstore owners, and librarians who have encouraged my efforts: I didn't think anybody read books anymore, thanks for proving me wrong. And to Dean Connors: thanks for the "map" (some think I write books just to benefit from the fine spread at the receptions he hosts for me).

The above individuals and organizations are not responsible for inaccurate conclusions, unfounded inferences, improper suggestions, unlikely factual settings, indecent allusions, or amoral and immoral content. The responsibility for any troubling or bizarre material lies solely within my interpretation of my sources' remarks.

Special appreciation is due Bill and Martha Boyer for the loan of the south of the border retreat where I organized this collection. *¡Muchas gracias!*

To Jerry Minnich and Prairie Oak Press: thanks for caring about Wisconsin's stories.

To Donna, Sam, and Ben: thanks for letting me play outside.

Introduction

One problem that arises when attempting to organize regional collections of stories is setting boundaries of a region. This is especially true of the vague concepts of the *northwoods* and the *north country.* Unlike the bioregion that I explored in *Driftless Spirits: Ghosts of Southwest Wisconsin*, there is no agreed upon definition of Wisconsin's northland.

There is much argument about where the north begins. Some Illinois vacationers would say it begins at Lake Geneva. Many hardcore loon chasers would say the dividing line is Highway 8 from Iron Mountain to St. Croix Falls. Stevens Point, Wausau, and Merrill all have their boosters as gateway-to-the-north communities. Truth be known, the traveler encounters hints of the northwoods such as the North Star Tavern only an hour north of Madison on Highway 51.

Such competitive jostling for northwoods status simply underscores the inadequacy of pure geography. The northwoods is as much a state of mind as it is a region. For some, the north begins where the prairie oaks give way to tamarack and jack pine. For others, the north evolves with shifting indicators; how far south wolves and bears roam these days.

The collector of stories must inevitably set limits and develop organizing concepts. My preference is to group stories with a strong sense of place. An interesting ghost story goes beyond apparitions in old houses—it speaks to the unique physical and cultural characteristics of a community. In Wisconsin, the stories inevitably draw upon the feelings of the first inhabitants. Those American Indian trailblazers knew that the Great Spirit was more accessible in certain places than in others.

Initially, I expected to use the techniques I developed with *Driftless Spirits* to compile a similar warm and fuzzy collection of ghost stories. Any differences, I suspected, would simply be a matter of shifting from the sleepy hollows of southwest Wisconsin's pastoral ridge country to the lake cottages north of 45 degrees latitude.

The task turned out to be more complicated than that and the stories far more difficult to classify. Northwoods ghost stories are not like the wistful tales of southwest Wisconsin's homesteading past. In the northwoods, a ghost story is more likely to be connected to grievances than to nostalgia. It is more likely to be associated with assorted strange phenomena and conspiracy theories than to classic American folklore motifs.

Perhaps ghost stories, like folklore classifications themselves, are too narrow to encompass everything that emerges in a multicultural society when established traditions collide with both New Age thinking and the politics of the New World Order. My naming of *Field of Dreams, Cold Mountain, Midnight in the Garden of Good and Evil,* and *Bridges of Madison County* as my favorite contemporary ghost stories surprises my friends. For me, a haunting usually comes down to the reverberations of the past in a way peculiar to a particular place.

In Wisconsin's northwoods, the stories bear many marks: old legends, internet exchange, political paranoia, spiritual revival, sturdy populism, ancient remedies, modern pharmaceuticals, science and science fiction. In this environment I found it impossible to compile a conventional collection of ghost stories. The things I heard required a broader approach. Thus, my presumption in calling this work a supernatural ecology.

Unlike the lazy and almost random decades-long collection of stories that produced my prior works, *Northern Frights* is the product of a more conscious journey. It drew heavily upon networks of fiercely independent people who spurred me onward. Never before had my sources seemed so convinced of the importance and urgency of understanding observed phenomena.

Like so many other of my recent journeys, this odyssey began among the stacks and map cases of Foundry Books in Mineral Point. It is an excellent place to delve into the information and cartography of the age of exploration in the Great Lakes area. Part bookstore, part museum, and part regional discussion salon, owner Dean Connors has lovingly created a place that is a shrine to the magical and adventurous parts of Wisconsin's past.

Because of this starting point, the stories are heavily influenced by the geographical metaphors. The first chapter explains how this journey began and how the area under consideration took shape. Keep your gazetteer and atlas handy as you read and explore northern Wisconsin through the pages of this book.

It is also important to note what this collection is not. It is not a compendium of haunted house stories in northern Wisconsin. It is not a survey of supernatural lore of the Great Lakes (that will come in another collection). It is not a thorough regional treatment of supernatural happenings in nearby areas of the Upper Peninsula of Michigan and the Minnesota lakeshore.

This collection is not an attempt to present a comprehensive review of American Indian spirit lore. The reader will note that sources are drawn from among all current Wisconsin tribes, a few displaced tribes, and a number of mixed and virtually extinguished tribal traditions. In tribal references, I deferred to my sources. I use the group names and spellings as they use them. Thus, one finds the terms Anishinabe, Objibwe, and Chippewa used to refer to the related groups which have reservations at Red Cliff, Bad River, Lac du Flambeau, Mole Lake, Turtle Lake, Lac Courte Orielles, and adjacent areas of Michigan, Minnesota, and Ontario.

The traditions or spiritual teachings mentioned in the narratives are presented solely to help understand the interpretations placed on unexplained phenomena by my sources. Their views on the sacred stories of their people do not always coincide with the recognized spiritual leaders of their communities.

None of the material related to dreams, ceremonies, healing, or contact with spirits should be viewed as a guide book. The practices described in these stories—be they American Indian, New Age, Wiccan, or Christian—are more involved than the narratives suggest. Those interested in such practices should contact experienced elders to seek guidance and training. Serious psychological and physical consequences can result from improper experimentation with these methods. As they say, do not try this at home.

Caution is also in order regarding readers' "field trips" to sites described in these stories. Publication of *Driftless Spirits* taught me the emerging practice of readers visiting the locations mentioned in ghost stories. While some of these sites are open to the public, many are not. Please respect the privacy of rural dwellers and seek permission before entering private property.

Long-term residents familiar with the odd happenings mentioned in these stories may know of other tales associated with the same sites. It is not uncommon in ghost lore to have predecessor tales or auxiliary tales at a common site. Indeed, some paranormal investigators suggest that the energy of an encounter with a spirit or other unexplained phenomena leads to a highly individualized experience. Readers are welcome to send additional details and observations about the manifestations and sites in this book to the author at the publisher's address.

Although this collection was compiled in almost record time compared to my prior plodding works, a great deal has changed about my sources and their situations. Quite a few have died, several have moved away, two are incarcerated, and one is the subject of a competency proceeding. The angry ones are angrier. In some cases, landscapes have changed with the coming of lakeshore developers and bulldozers.

True to the predictions made by those who served as my guides and mentors, many of the sources for these tales proved eccentric and passionate. While not always agreeing with their diagnosis of events, I found myself surprised at the affection I felt for these irritable nonconformists. I hope they will forgive any excesses wrongly attributed to their characters.

This project comes to close on a starless winter's eve of wind and whipping snow. The cold storm howl is coming straight down Wisconsin off Lake Superior. Yet these pages bring a warmth back to my heart as I recall the journey: the northern lights, the cozy cabins, the deep woods, the hidden lakes, and the now told untold mysteries.

Meegwetch,

Dennis Boyer
Town of Linden
Iowa County, Wisconsin
January 7, 1998

Explanatory Notes

I use the term "ghost story" in a broader fashion than most who write about spirits and hauntings. Those expecting a reprise of my first collection, *Driftless Spirits: Ghosts of Southwest Wisconsin*, will be surprised but, I hope, not disappointed.

I continue to approach my subject matter with a strong sense of place. In addition, I use the same sorts of cultural and ethnic benchmarks that marked the folklore mood of my second book, *Giants in the Land: Folk Tales and Legends of Wisconsin*. I look for magic in the most mundane of circumstances.

Northern Frights goes a step further. By closely listening to the incredible stories of northern Wisconsin residents, I attempt to provide an overview of all manner of bizarre claims and alleged sightings. As odd as some tales may seem, each is based on accounts provided by my sources.

These accounts are not just ghost stories. The book is a treatment of virtually all things outside of what we usually call normal and natural. Thus, a rather traditional ghost story might be, from the sources' perspective, a combination of the impacts of aliens and secret technology and involve travel through time, space, and other dimensions. The sources' analytical framework for explaining their experiences may draw upon well-established spiritual traditions or may flow from individually created systems.

Readers should understand that this book is a literary and interpretive work. These narratives are not unabridged anthropological field notes nor verbatim folklore interview transcripts. The identities of narrators are concealed and, except for a few public sites, the locations are purposely left vague.

In some cases, composite narrators have been created to deal with the problem of disclosures from multiple sources. In such cases, care was taken to merge their observations in ways that respect the experiences and reflect the voices of the sources. A number of historical figures are referred to in the context of established events. Other characters are constructed in the narratives to take the place of innocent bystanders deserving of privacy.

I withhold my feelings about my sources' mental states and motivations. I am content to let the narratives speak for themselves.

PART I

Lake Superior Slope

Point of the Beginning

Wisconsin *stories of the American pioneer era usually have a link to southwest Wisconsin. European-American settlement first marched into the Wisconsin territory by way of the Mississippi River. The geopolitical influence of English Canada and French-speaking Quebec on northern Wisconsin was brought to a close by this invasion.*

The old centers of La Pointe, La Baye, and Prairie du Chien were soon eclipsed by the new settlements of Belmont, Mineral Point, and Hamilton Diggings (present day Wiota). The settlement pattern assured the political, economic, and cultural dominance of southern Wisconsin. The Bad Axe massacre at the conclusion of the Black Hawk War sent a strong message to the northern tribes. Even the first formal survey of Wisconsin commenced with a "point of the beginning" near Hazel Green, which established the baseline for the cartographic ranges and towns seen on our plat maps.

Since those days, Wisconsin has undergone many changes. Southwest Wisconsin lost its political influence and the cities of southeast Wisconsin and the Fox Valley came to the fore. Northern Wisconsin did not always benefit from periods of prosperity—even when its resources fueled wider growth. Many residents of the northwoods describe their relationship with the rest of Wisconsin in terms of cycles of neglect and exploitation.

After Driftless Spirits, *it was my intent to work on other collections of Upper Midwest ghost stories. A handful of novel tales from the northwoods came my way and sent me out scouting for more.*

But it was not until I encountered a former Minocqua resident in Mineral Point's Foundry Books that I began to see that the tone of this collection would differ dramatically from my prior work. Blake inquired about my next book project. When he heard that the focus was on northwoods ghosts, he gave me a sly smile. Before long the Oneida County transplant turned Wisconsin Department of Justice investigator had me looking at the task in an entirely different light.

Don't think you're going to drive around northern Wisconsin and traipse down driveways and stick your head in shacks looking for ghost

3

stories. If you want to hear the really weird stuff, you'll skip the well-known grandpops in rocking chairs and focus in on the people nobody listens to.

There's a lot of anger up there. Locals who distrust outsiders. People who moved up there because modern life stressed them out. People who see plots in everything and think every government action has a sinister motive. They sense the breakdown of community and the threats to the environment and aren't sure what to do about it.

You have lots of folks who live alone. Really alone. With lots of quiet to hear things and see things. People who get in touch with their senses and instincts. If they tell you they saw a ghost or a UFO or sweep team of federal agents, well, they saw something. They're not looking for attention.

There are lots of haunted places and haunted people up there. Don't be put off just because they're cranky and odd. Don't write them off just because they see evil in places you can't.

Maybe it's not a matter of pure evil. Maybe it's an imbalance where goodness and light are losing the fight. Maybe it's the simple psychic energy of all the dissatisfaction.

Let's face it, the northwoods is filled with dissatisfaction. It's just not as idyllic as most hope for. It's often a hard life. And hard lives are often lives of anger, resentment, envy, and even paranoia. Yes, maybe it clouds their judgment about who's responsible for their problems. But I don't think it makes them scared of things that go bump in the night. Hell, most of the people I know would just like to bump back.

I'll concede there's a bit of a victim mentality up there. So when there's a strange creature lurking or an evil force in operation, it's the fault of the whole world. They are certain that they live in an extraction zone that is used to feed our mall gods of the great consumer religion. They flatter themselves that they're in the only such zone. They forget the Kickapoo Valley, the Baraboo Bluffs, the lower Wisconsin River, much less the Amazon or Alaska's northern slope.

After you connect with some of these folks, you'll see that their whole view of the supernatural is tangled up in their personal angles on government, business, politics, and religion. With most of the real anger reserved for the twin conspiracies of government and business. Politics and religion are just the tools that are used to fight the battles.

From their perspective, government is a paranormal phenomena. Think about it, if you believe in individual sovereignty and the natural rights of man, then government looks as irrational and mysterious as some goofy cult. If you have a strong sense of self, then government can't seem real.

The paranormal view of government is the product of our era where the sole function of government is deception. It specializes in the mirror-to-mirror imaging that has you looking into a stupor-inducing infinity. It's a type of magic.

So when the government says there are no UFOs it holds infinite meanings. Do they believe that there are none? Or only that they don't want you to believe? Or that they want you to disbelieve their denials? Or does it mean there are UFOs, but they're not what they seem and the denials get people looking in the wrong direction? See what I mean?

Even the right-wing, anti-government types have a deference to government that borders on a hypnotic state. They serve in its army, back its law enforcement, and then claim the whole thing is a plot. They can't seem to sort out wacko nationalism from genuine patriotism.

See, I think nationalism is a type of devil worship. The idea of a state in control of people's lives may be worse than a satanic cult. It's certainly killed more people over time. They base their control on so-called protection, but we need protection from them. You could turn loose all the sociopaths, psychotics, and serial killers for fifty years and they couldn't begin to cause the violence and suffering caused in the name of government.

You won't get a real line on a genuine northwoods story about strange stuff from an official source. Doesn't matter whether it's the DNR, the Wisconsin Manufacturers and Commerce, or the Sierra Club. They all have a proprietary tone about northern Wisconsin, but they're not of it.

Talk to the misfits and people on the margins. Talk to the old hermits in the backwoods. Find the women who howl at the moon and scare the neighbors. And talk to the Indians: the old wise men, the young hotheads, and stable women who keep business going. There are stories of weird things up there. I'll give you some contacts to get you started. Once you're in the network, you'll just roll along.

You'll know you're on the right track when you find the people who don't know where they end and where their little speck of God's Country begins. Their sense of spirits, the supernatural, and the just

5

plain weird is what I would call *locational.* What they have to say will be rooted in the dirt, swamp, or water that's important to them.

A fellow could probably map out these strange tales. There might be a system to this stuff, some patterns, or some links between these things. One thing for sure, when you're done, you'll know just how different a northwoods ghost story is from its paler cousins in southern Wisconsin.

The Old One

*Ghosts are abundant in all forms of collective human memory.
They fill the annals of folklore and inhabit the lyrics of song. They echo
in oral traditions and linger in poetry. Even history's footnotes pay
them tribute.*

*Wisconsin is fertile ghost territory. The ghost stories of the pio-
neer lead miners and the pre-Civil War homesteaders provide a rich
texture to the folktales of the southern third of Wisconsin.*

*North country ghosts are less well known for a number of reasons.
Later settlement and distance from population centers are factors.
Other factors include the origins of so many north country ghosts
among unfamiliar groups: Ojibwe, Menominee, Finn, French Canadian, Icelandic, and so forth.*

*This collection is organized in such a way that this story must come
first as Wisconsin's northernmost localized ghost. A number of other
Lake Superior spirits have left their mark, but they may be claimed
more properly by the Upper Peninsula of Michigan or by Ontario.*

*More surprising is the story's rank as Wisconsin's oldest ghost tale.
But perhaps it is fitting that the story is placed in Wisconsin's prehistory of pristine water and ice.*

*It is, of course, a fisherman's tale. The setting is the source's boat,
a midsized craft down-rigged for salmon and lake trout. The craft is
headed northeast out of Cornucopia toward a "secret spot." A look at
a map shows the destination to be at the "top" of Wisconsin. Clay lets
us tag along for the ride.*

〰 〰 〰

Lots of secrets in this lake for those who take the time to know
them. There's more to a lake than shoreline and navigational aids. More
than small-craft warnings and weather reports. First off, a fisherman
must know the bottom of the lake. Where the underwater ridges,
trenches, junk cars, and sunken ships are. Get to know those things as
well as you know which marinas have clean gas and cold beer.

Then you got to know the layers of the lake. The sub-surface currents. The temperature differences at different depths. Finally you need
to understand the mystery of the lake. Respect its power, its spirit.

Know it as a living thing. Listen to its lessons. Let it flow right through you. Now there's equipment, gadgets, and gizmos to help you with those first two things. But the last thing has got to be in you. If you can look out on a sparkling Lake Superior and fail to get any sense of mystery, magic, and majesty—well, then you're a lost cause.

All the big bodies of water have ghosts in them. Hundreds, thousands, maybe millions of souls lost in the depths. Lake Superior is loaded with them. Shipwrecks, war parties lost in storms, fishermen gone mad. Not to mention the various haunted lighthouses, piers, and breakwaters. But you can get a sense that each one is linked to a specific event. Things that can be found in history or at least in Chippewa stories.

It's different with the one I call "the old one." There's a depth there you got to feel in your gut or heart. Instruments won't work on this type of thing. I first saw him—maybe I should say I first experienced him—three miles due north of Outer Island. A golden early morning fog was about to lift.

The old one spoke to me without saying a word. Mental telepathy, I guess. A feeling that you were being filled up with something. Like a big bowl of good soup. He let me know he was the first soul claimed by Lake Superior. An old, old soul. From a time when maybe people weren't quite people like we think of them today.

He was from a time before the tribes. Maybe before races or ethnic groups as we know them. He was a lone journeyer. The hunter or scout of humankind's prehistory who found the new lands. The ones who located the herds. The ones who bravely crossed great bodies of water on improvised boats or rafts.

It was that type of journey that claimed him. One of those famous early autumn storms. A day that started with blue sky and blue water and ended with towering gray water and a scudding gray sky. He would have been the first to cross Lake Superior. He was within sight of the Apostle Islands. He would have been the first human to set foot in what is now Wisconsin.

His spirit has been out there a long time. Ten, twenty thousand years. What's time to a ghost? He's different from other lake ghosts in one important respect. He's not a tortured soul. Not someone tormented by his ordeal.

His spirit is still filled with the exhilaration of the powerful lake. Still filled with the awe of Creation and his connection to it. He's reconciled to his status. He didn't go down with a grimace or a wail. No, when he went under it was with a celebratory howl.

The Chipp boatmen at Red Cliff know of him. The commercial fishermen know him. He's appeared to iron ore ships, grain ships, and even weekend sailboaters. When my Red Cliff buddies and I went up to Ontario we found Canadian Chipps east of Thunder Bay who knew the story. They called him "guardian of the waters."

It's a good name. He's been that in ways I didn't understand at first. The first thing that comes to mind is the obvious thought that he is protector of lake sailors. Well, that he is. He's helped many craft around the islands in poor visibility. He's guided boats into Cornucopia, Port Wing, and Red Cliff.

He saved me as I tried to race a storm home. I couldn't see zilch. Rain coming down buckets. He appeared on the water right in front of me, rising and falling with the swells. Naturally I swerved. And lucky I did. He no sooner appeared than the shoreline rocks loomed out of the gray.

He's often seen like that. Walking calmly on the water in the worst storms. Although I've heard of him running across the dark waters at night with a torch. Those tales go way, way back. Back past the Chipps. Maybe past the times of the Hurons and Menominees on the big lake. I don't think there is an older ghost story in all of North America.

But all that can obscure the other side of the old one. Kind of reduces him to the status of a navigational beacon or buoy. When the Canadian Chipps said he guards the big lake it means more than correcting errors of seamanship. He is a guardian of the big lake and of all the waters.

I was a bit slow to recognize this. But as I found him speaking to me while on the lake he touched something in me that made me understand that this water is life itself. You know we have people who still remember when this water was pure enough to drink untreated. It wasn't long ago that we didn't have widespread PCBs or mercury fallout from coal-burning power plants.

The old one put it in my heart to make a fuss about things. Things like contamination in fish and papermills and the military's poison barrels at the bottom of the lake. We've got a lot of people up here on the Lake Superior shore who've been touched by this spirit. Who share a vision of the big lake as an old and wild thing.

When you ask about north country ghosts, you ask a big question. You got to go past haunted shanties and lights in windows. Go to the

9

essence of the north country. Go to its water. Water is the story of the north country. Hell, it's the story of Wisconsin. It's what people crossed to get here. It's our draw even today.

So start with the old one. Start north of Outer Island on a late October or early November day with a rising northern wind pushing gray ahead of it. Listen close. Listen in that wind for his celebratory howl. Howl with it!

Manitou Island Bad Boys

North country ghost tales draw heavily upon American Indian oral traditions. It is not surprising that the first dry land ghost in this collection would emerge from that direction. It is even less surprising that the source would be Chippewa. The real surprise about the story is its contemporary context. Chippewa storytelling is blessed with many traditional tales with ancient roots. Modern day angles in these stories are not common.

The events described here hint at the continued sense of the sacred within the community. But they also reveal some of the conflicts over who "owns" the oral traditions and whether they can be added to by new generations. The community is the Red Cliff Reservation. A look at a map shows it to be Wisconsin's northernmost organized settlement. It offers Wisconsin's northernmost cluster of haunted houses in the form of abandoned vacation homes.

Our source here enjoys people-watching at the Red Cliff bowling alley/casino/tavern. He sits for hours watching the drama unfold while sipping pop. He finds amusement in both the bumbling of the tourists and the bickering of tribal officials. On this night the entertainment is sparse. A wandering conversation fills the gap: hunting, fishing, the weather, and strange experiences. The latter topic draws a confession from Crawford.

I never thought I would talk about ghosts. But then I never thought I would see any ghosts. It was not what I expected.

You see I was brought up here on the rez[1] with a steady diet of traditional stories about the Great Spirit, Wendigos, and Wenebojo. I never heard a spiritual teacher or medicine man talk about ghosts like those in a horror movie. No, there are special spirits for almost every place and for every type of activity.

We never had that much of a tradition about haunted spots. But then I don't know everything and I'm not close to the traditionalists. My talk of ghosts really got me into trouble with the traditionalists. Maybe it's because of the friction it uncovered. By that I mean disagreements within the tribe.

It all started when I took the boys around the islands in canoes. The plan was to go around the bottom of Basswood, up to Stockton and meet the parents at a camp on Oak. But when you've got a bunch of boys, plans don't mean much. When we got up to Stockton the boys wanted to walk around. So we got out at the west trail on Quarry Bay. I told them they shouldn't go far. Famous last words, right?

Well I could tell you a two-hour story about what happened on Stockton Island. But if you have kids or have ever taken care of a bunch of kids, you can use your imagination. The bottom line was that some of the boys got lost. They got off the trail. It took the better part of the day to round them up. You know how it is with boys, though. You find one, you lose two.

Then we got the canoes around to the other side of the island to pick up the stragglers. I was just hoping it wouldn't be too dark by the time we got back. Out in the channel the next problem developed. A wind came up out of the southwest. We couldn't make any headway: The boys were tired and two of the canoes blew back toward Manitou Island.

If nothing else had happened I still would have had eight parents angry at me for not getting the boys to the Oak Island camp. Instead we ended up spending the night on Manitou Island. And what a night!

First we had a storm hit. Lightning and high winds. We couldn't get a fire started. We couldn't get a tarp up. Then around midnight the storm broke. A fat moon peeked through the clouds while we got a fire going. That perked the boys up. Especially since we could now see lights and fires on Oak Island. Everything would be fine in the morning.

---

[1]reservation

11

But then we started to see something else. Boys started running by us. First in ones and twos. Then by fives and sixes. They all had their hair long. But they were dressed in different ways. Some naked, some with just a cloth around their middles, and some in deerskin shirts. They whooped and hollered. In the bushes we heard laughter. Somewhere there was singing and a drum.

My boys sat around the fire with eyes wide open. No one said a word. They all knew that they were seeing ghosts. This went on for maybe ten minutes. It seems hundreds of boys went by. But who knows? Maybe it was the same couple of dozen running in a circle.

Back on the rez the story stirred things up. Some of the oldtimers thought I did something wrong out on Manitou Island. Maybe I did stir up some spirits. But I asked for advice. Then I went out to Manitou Island to set things right. I burned sage, white cedar, and tobacco out there.

The oldtimers described it all on one level. It was because someone ignored the power of the manitou. The old men talked about angry manitouk—that's more than one manitou—and about how the manitouk are connected to our place in the Creation.

But I found out the women have a different angle on this. My aunt told me that old women always talked about the spirits of naughty boys. She said there've always been young shinnobs[2] who had to run off on adventures. She said that even before the old wars with the Sioux that young Chipp men would disappear on such adventures. They thought it was only natural that those wayward souls would gather and play and make mischief.

She got into this bad boy theme so much I could see that Ojibwe women must feel let down by men in some respects. So what the oldtimers talked of as the spiritual journey she saw as a bunch of running around. I guess it's made more complicated by the differences between the traditionalists and the Christians. They don't exactly see ghosts and spirits the same way.

But where I got the most grief was from some of the tribal officials. They're always on the business angle. How is this going to affect tourism? Will it keep people away from the casino? They even said I might cause problems with the state and the feds. Somehow they

---

[2]This term is short for Anishinabe, the dialect self-designation of the Chippewa or Ojibee.

thought that the DNR and the National Park Service would pick a fight over ghosts.

But I learned a lot through all this. I learned that the tribe is a big squabbling family. But the arguments should never wipe out the fact that it is a family and that all parts of the family have a role. We need all the parts and all their interpretations to figure things out.

I learned a lot about how you white guys look at us Indians. Everybody from the goofy New Agers to the Indian haters thinks we have some special hocus-pocus to sort out mysteries. They don't want to see that there are different ways of seeing things and doing things among us.

What did I learn about ghosts? Well, that's complicated, too. Yes, there are ghosts out on Manitou Island. Yes, it does appear that the ghosts are a bunch of hell-raising boys.

But I've gone out to Manitou Island a bunch of times. I've studied them. I've asked questions—like the oldtimers say, "in the right way." Which means humility, honesty, and modesty along with following the procedures. I've reached the conclusion that the ghosts out there are just like us over here. Their backgrounds are complicated. Their roles are different from each other. But they are a family in a way.

When I fasted out there I got the feeling it was kind of a cosmic stew. Sort of a Rod Serling, Bermuda Triangle sort of thing. A lot of it must go back to the fights for Lake Superior. The wars with the Sioux. The fights between the Menominee and the Sac. The battles between the Winnebago and the Fox. Even the fur wars after the British and the French came.

In a way the wars didn't penetrate that other reality of Manitou Island. Boys get to stay boys there. That's the appeal, I think. The eternal youth. There's an undercurrent that maybe some oldtimers go out there when their time has come to pass over. I hope to find out some day whether I can get back to those wild boyhood times.

Write it down. I'll be the one streaking bare-butt past the cooking fire.

Herbster's Phantom Pulp Truck

Ghost vehicles and their drivers are fairly common out on the old U.S. routes of the Great Plains and down on the twisting hollow roads of Appalachia. But Wisconsin seems to lack a classic ghost trucker of the type immortalized in country and western song.

Ridgeway in Iowa County has its ghostly motorcycles. Lafayette County has some phantom farm equipment. The length of the Kettle Moraine area boasts tales of spirit-operated pickup trucks.

Yet there appears to be nothing like the archetypal phantom semi with a story of a deadly collision brought on by heroic efforts to avoid a loaded school bus. Wisconsin always has a different angle.

This is especially true in the quirky and stubborn community of Herbster. While Herbster is not much more than a few streets intersecting with Highway 13, it has the antiestablishment mood of the Kickapoo Valley and the economic anger of Milwaukee's urban core.

Herbster and the surrounding town of Clover have been focal points for dissatisfaction since the late 1970s. The U.S. Navy's extremely low frequency (ELF) radio antenna and the on-again off-again radioactive waste disposal plans provide a context for local suspicions and resentments.

Through many of these years it was customary to gather at Luttman's Tavern in Herbster to air grievances and hatch political plots. There, the county board supervisor, town board members, and ecology activists conducted open forums. They fielded complaints ranging from problems at the town dump to rage at the state and federal sting operation directed at commercial fishermen. Not surprisingly, many of the gripes came from loggers and log haulers.

On one particular day the complaints centered on pulp prices, logging hazards, and the condition of the forest roads in the Chequamegon National Forest. One trucker, Cal, threw an off-beat item into the mix.

🌿 🌿 🌿

I got something different for you. About a half-dozen trucks were run off roads south of here. Mostly on Lenawee Road. But one down on Battle Axe Road. Last week it happened less than a mile from here

14

at the intersection of Lenawee and Busche Town Road. Couple of the boys busted up rigs real bad.

What was screwy about the whole deal was that each trucker claimed that the rig what ran them off was an older truck. Yeah, a truck maybe thirty or forty years old. Yeah, an old-time pulp truck.

Well, that got me interested. Ya know I've been hauling since I was a kid. Started with my dad right after the war. So I saw all the old rigs. Yeah, when I started we were still loading by hand. No hydraulic claws, no booms. Just some crossbred horses and a jammer to help load.

So back to the old truck. I thought to myself I'd like to see the dirty so-and-so. Maybe run him off the road! Well, darn if I didn't see it. Just after dark. He zoomed right out of Seven Mile Road. The so-and-so ran his rig right across the road and into the trails on the west side. Darn if I could figure where that truck went. Ya can't drive a pick-up through there, much less anything big.

Now the truck itself, that was a sight. It was a faded old GMC 450. My best guess is a 1954 tandem with the 302-cubic-inch straight-six engine. I know that type well. We had one. Ya know, in the fifties you could get a straight truck for two thousand bucks. Then tandems came out and you were looking at eight grand. And that wasn't even customized for pulp. No, for that ya had to go to a local blacksmith.

But I noticed something more important then the truck and it was something no one else had mentioned. The darn thing didn't have a driver! Yeah! You and I know that the drunks, crackpots, and woods hippies see all sorts of things. Or at least think they do. We've heard it all. Ghosts, UFOs, whales in the lake, ya name it.

Yeah, yeah, I know about the Russian ghosts in Cornucopia and the fishermen spirits on the lake. But ya always think of these things as just stories. Even when the old farts swear by them. But what the heck, why shouldn't I ask one of the old farts? So I did. I asked old Ollie down in Iron River. He lives down there now with his daughter.

He told me there were two things going on here. One was the pulp truck itself. The other was something on Lewanee Road, right around Lake Lewanee. He said there's been a pulp truck roaming the logging roads for forty years. Darn if I ever heard about it! But old Ollie said it's been out there.

According to Ollie no one really knows the deal on the truck. No one remembers anyone dying in a pulp truck accident around there.

So if someone was killed no one is talking about it. Or maybe it was a stranger working for an outside outfit.

Now the Lake Lewanee stuff is a little harder to explain. Ollie said there were stories of a ghost there for years. Not the usual floating bed-sheet ghost. No, a rip-snorter that scared old loggers and the Chippewa talked about it years ago. Stuff about people going crazy, cannibalism, and mutilation.

Old Ollie had some strange ideas about all of this. He said that the navy ELF thing disturbs the magnetic field. That and some hidden nuclear waste depositories. Said it messes up the ghosts and riles them like something up the butt.

Now Ollie didn't dream this science stuff up on his own. He said some professor came around to ask about the pulp truck. Although Ollie's daughter said the guy looked too sleazy to be a professor. This professor told Ollie that disturbed ghosts can consolidate powers. And if there's one really rotten S.O.B. ghost he can take over the show and use other ghosts. Supposedly that's what's happening with the pulp truck. The Lake Lewanee thing is now at the wheel.

Ollie said this professor had a map of spirits that cause problems like this. Did ya ever hear of such a crazy thing? The things these college guys piss away money on! But something's definitely out of whack. When I saw the pulp truck again last night it got to me as much as anything ever has. Maybe it's time to quit drinking.

This time I heard terrific screams and groans. And instead of pulp logs on the truck I saw chained-down bodies. Whatcha going to do about that?

The Old La Pointe Ghosts

Wisconsin ghosts offer a number of familiar forms: hunters, fishermen, and early settlers. Perhaps the most widespread, both in terms of geography and quantity, is the gathering of rough pioneer ghosts. Helena's rowdy ghosts in Iowa County were the first group of such *ghosts that I encountered in my story collection efforts. Those ghosts were clearly voyagers and trappers of the pre-Black Hawk War period.*

It turned out that virtually every area with some evidence of pioneer gathering had such ghosts. This included most of the early tavern, trading post, and rendezvous sites. The stories of such ghost gatherings fall in three main corridors. The Fox River from Green Bay to Portage is thick with such sightings. The Mississippi River has quite a few from Trempealeau south to Potosi. The Wisconsin River sample spans from Eagle River to Blue River.

So what makes the old La Pointe ghosts unique? That was initially a hard question to answer. On the surface they were very much like the other groups of pioneer ghosts.

My guide thought the old La Pointe ghosts had a special place in Wisconsin's pantheon of spirits. She saw them as fully developed personalities. But she also thought of them as "foundation ghosts" or ghosts with linkages to sightings and stories elsewhere.

The isolated settings of cabins, taverns, boat landings, bait shops and kitchen tables provided the environments for most ghost stories in Wisconsin. But this story unfolded while my guide was on the move. She allowed me to accompany her through a busy day that included waitressing, volunteer work, a ferry ride, a tour of a museum, and a walk in Big Bay State Park.

The day started with strong black coffee in a Bayfield cafe and ended with the smell of the Gruenke's Inn fish boil. In between it was a day of shouted breakfast orders, pinging mast lines, crying gulls, shoving tourists, and Jeannette's running commentary.

🔥 🔥 🔥

Madeline Island is a ghost haven. Or maybe a ghost heaven? Isn't it heaven up here for at least four or five months a year?

When I wrote you a letter about the old La Pointe ghosts I couldn't really put into words everything I was thinking about. I wanted you to hear it all from me and judge whether or not I'm crazy. Only one person in a hundred around here will admit to seeing a ghost. I'm that one in a hundred.

We're not supposed to talk about anything that might keep the tourists out. And if you talk about some of the people who went nuts or drank themselves to death because of what they saw, well, you don't run that in your ad in the Minneapolis papers.

We have beauty up here. But these ghosts show that things are out of balance and very fragile. The old La Pointe ghosts own the streets of La Pointe after dark. They can show themselves as pretty horrid creatures when they want to.

Usually they show themselves first as oldtimers in deerskin coats and fur hats. Nothing too scary about that. But just when they get people looking, they turn ugly. The last time I saw them I looked just a little too long. Next thing I knew I was looking at melting flesh dripping off bones.

Now these ghosts are most often seen right along the main street and down to the ferry landing. Sometimes they'll be carrying on right outside the museum. I help out in the museum. The other ladies wouldn't like me to say this, but there are many things in the museum that keep the ghosts stirred up.

Not only the old La Pointe ghosts, but the others on Madeline Island, too. We've got others on Black Shanty Road, at Big Bay Lagoon, at Amnicon Point, and at Sunset Bay.

But I think they're all related to the old La Pointe ghosts. They're the foundation ghosts. They're from those old French families that left their mark all over Wisconsin. An old man told me that when they're not here they can pop up in Green Bay, Prairie du Chien, and anywhere else they have ties to.

I won't go into which families we're talking about. They get real touchy about that history. The ghosts themselves are quite distinct. I can even see the physical and personality resemblances to their families today.

There's the Red Beard. A big quiet fellow. Wears a blue cap. He always looks toward the lake when he's on land. But during the winter he sometimes wanders on the ice. We have Hook Nose. A skinny devil with an earring. Has a crimson sash and a dagger. Looks like a pirate.

Then there's Long Jacques. He's the one with the gleaming eyes and the pistols in his belt. He is known to follow women and peep in windows. There are others, too. The usual types. Trappers, traders, woodsmen, soldiers, deserters. I can go into them all another time.

But there's the one that really seems to stand out. Maybe he's the ringleader. Or maybe he's just a guide. Sometimes it seems like he's alive, more of a devil than a ghost. He's the old one-eyed man with the cackling laugh. We have something that belonged to him on display in the museum. I'd like to get it out of there. We might get some peace that way.

18

But I don't dare take it out. Especially after what happened with that sacred stone or rock spirit. We had this stone in the museum that the Chippewa said had something to do with their religion. I really don't understand what it was all about.

But the medicine man or whatever said he needed it for a ceremony. So we loaned it to him. But he didn't bring it back. Said he buried it in the woods on the northeast end of the island. Good Lord, did the talk get nasty around the museum. It was Indians this and Indians that and threats to stay out of the casinos.

But we're better off without it. I think we're safer without it. There was something odd about it. A buzzing sound if you were in a room with it alone. I think those ghosts drew energy off of it.

There's that whole problem that we have of stolen artifacts, disturbed graves, and building on top of earlier sacred sites. It's one of the reasons things are out of balance. Then there are the other things that were taken. Iron and copper out of the ground. All the big trees out of the woods. You can't tell me that doesn't affect the energy of a place.

Look at the symptoms. Lampreys and mussels in the lake. Birds, animals, and plants dying off. And there's the human side. Yes, there's a connection between the injury to nature and the injury to our communities. Values are slipping away and strange behavior is increasing. It's not just crime, although there's plenty of that. It's the sick things done to children. The sick, sick mutilations.

I firmly believe that every time the old La Pointe ghosts make a big fuss there's some bad thing that happens the same night.

When you think about it, most of our ghosts aren't really scary. Maybe they should be. Maybe they were meant to be. Maybe it's another sign that life is out of balance that real life is scarier than ghosts. Our ghosts are so colorful. Our real life human monsters usually turn out to be so ordinary. Maybe there's a connection there.

Those old La Pointe ghosts are connected to something a fisherman told me about Lac Vieux Desert. When you get down there you'll hear about a tear in the curtain between heaven and earth. Ghosts are pouring through it. Some think it's funny or at least interesting. I think it shows something is wrong.

It was kind of quaint when the old La Pointe ghosts just stayed on Madeline Island and scared children. Now they show up two or three hundred miles away near bodies in swamps and ditches. There's something definitely wrong with that.

Ghosts of the Three Fires

Thousands upon thousands of Wisconsinites have driven up U.S. Highway 2 to Ashland without noticing their passage through the Bad River Reservation. European-Americans know very little about their Ojibwe neighbors. They are usually lumped together as "those Chippewa up North" and linked in negative phrases to spearfishing and casino gambling.

Few Wisconsin residents know anything at all about the Bad River Chippewa and their links to legend and lore in the upper Great Lakes. It is the tribe of skilled lake fishermen, careful wild rice gatherers, nimble loggers, and gifted storytellers.

Fewer still know that the reservation village of Odanah is home to an inter-tribal agency called the Great Lakes Indian Fish and Wildlife Commission. The commission runs fish hatcheries, employs biologists and wardens, manages resources, studies ecology, and otherwise looks out for Mother Nature in the northern third of Wisconsin.

The commission is housed in an old school building on a loop road off of Highway 2. The headquarters is more than a center for research and enforcement. It is sometimes a gathering place for ecologists, naturalists, students, and curious non-Indians. In cold winter months it is a place for stories.

Our storyteller stops by often to "check out the rumor mill." Like a lot of Ojibwe men in their forties, he has seen the "white world" through military service, college, and professional employment. Like many of his contemporaries, his return to the reservation to raise children has led to a challenging juggle of dealings with tribal government, Ashland County government, and spiritual traditionalists. Still, Arlen's voice possesses the cadence of warm chuckling.

🌿 🌿 🌿

We Ojibwe have been surprising white guys with stories for a long time. Old Henry Schoolcraft—the Indian agent in territorial days—married an Ojibwe woman and was astounded to find out we had stories. He even wrote in his journal that we might have intellects and souls.

Bad River was always a crossroads for stories. It was the first major settlement—other than islands—when our people moved down out of Canada. Only Sault Saint Marie up in Michigan was a bigger center for the three fires or gathering of the Ojibwe, Ottawa, and Potawatomi. These were cousin groups who acted as an alliance and shared much of the same storytelling tradition.

I can only tell you this story because I was given tobacco now that the frog and the snake are frozen in the ground. They are bad spirits and should not hear stories which they could use for magic.

The "ghosts of the three fires" story is not a traditional story. Like many things, it is shaped by new knowledge and experiences. Some see the three fires as the Trinity. Some see it as the foundation for a new political alliance to be led by a new Tecumseh or Black Hawk.

Each of the three nations is linked to one of the ghosts. The Potawatomi ghost is the little brother. The Ottawa are the keepers of knowledge. The Ojibwe are the warriors. These three ghosts come from one of the last of the old three fires gatherings held at Bad River. It was a time when war could have come this way as had happened to the Sac and the Shawnee.

It was the moon of the falling leaves. It was time for the fall medicine dance. A time for relatives to come together for one last social occasion before the winter hunt. These were spiritual events because of the ceremonies. But there was also feasting, games, and storytelling.

The fall medicine dance was the time for the telling of stories about Wenebojo and windigos. In the fall they did not tell stories of spirits or manitou. That was for winter. At this gathering for the fall medicine dance there was a lot of nervousness. Prophets were talking about hard times to come. There was concern about war.

The chiefs decided to use this opportunity to test their young men. So there was competition in wrestling, shooting, and canoeing and so forth. But the biggest competition was the long race from the east bank of the Bad River to Superior Falls and back. Over twenty miles round-trip on rough trail.

Even though the other contests more clearly demonstrated warrior skills, the long run was most important to all the people. The skilled runners were the ones who brought news of invasion, stories of battle, and reports on casualties days before fighters returned. The top runner was highly honored.

In this race, all the young men ran. But each of the fires—Ojibwa, Ottawa, and Potawatomi—had a standout runner. Bets were made on the outcome in the spirit of friendly rivalry. These three main runners were actually good friends. They had often run together at three fires gatherings.

This day they were each made serious by the bets and by the dire prophecies of the medicine men. They each expected victory. They soon left the main body of racers far behind. They ran like they had never run before. Each tried to run along side the others so as to be in position to pull away should the others falter.

But the trail was narrow, so this meant a lot of jostling. Soon it turned to pushing and shoving. Soon they were hitting each other with fists. They ran and ran. But instead of the joy that comes with running hard, they were instead filled with the bitterness and hate that comes with wanting personal victory too much.

They soon were close to the finish. People on the bank of the Bad River could see them. Veins were popped out on the necks and faces of the runners. Their breathing was so heavy that it sounded like the rising storm. Red foam ran from their mouths.

They all dropped only feet from the finish. They were dead. They had run without spirit in their hearts and so it killed their hearts. Naturally the medicine men saw plenty of bad omens in all this. But the interpretation I stick with is the lesson of cooperation.

The three runners should have recognized that they were all champions. The honor was already theirs for being the best of each of their nations. The nations of the three fires were supposed to help each other. All Indian people are supposed to help each other. So now we have the ghosts of the three fires to remind us of that.

Their ghostly moonlight runs are different from their selfish competition in life. Now they urge each other on. They sing a song praising each other and praising the Indian way. And they still run to bring warnings. They run to tell when there is illegal toxic dumping going on. They run to tell us about Ashland County deputies filling Ojibwe arrest quotas.

And they can be running to tell us about evil spirits. About a growing evil and growing danger. This is all within our traditions even though we do not usually speak of ghosts. It is said that Bad River is noted on early maps as a place of active spirits.

Of the four original brothers in our creation story, Wauboozoo is the one I most identify with this place. He was the originator of music, dream quests, and prayer. He was also the first one to talk to the manitous and the first to come back as a ghost.

He was given the job of controlling the other ghosts and sending ghosts like the ghosts of the three fires on important missions. But there is reason to think his authority is being undermined by that growing evil I spoke of.

You will hear different explanations and different stories about this problem. I don't know what to make of what the Ackley family says. Our bingo faction thinks that the threat will come in the form of attacks on gambling. Our spearers think that it is our treaty rights which must be defended. The tribal officials worry about U.S. Congress and the Bureau of Indian Affairs. Maybe it is all those things. But maybe it is much more.

It is my hope that we will again learn to talk to the manitous. We used to view them as friends. And we knew Kitchi-Manitou as the Creator of all things. I think the ghosts of the three fires are meant to lead us back on the Creator's path. That is the preparation we need for the coming fight between those who stand with creation and those who would destroy it.

I predict that these running ghosts will be seen further and further away from here. They will help spread the word about the dangers that face us and about the cleansing time that will follow. Maybe after that the three fires will become the many fires.

The Phantom Lovers of Big Manitou Falls

Waterfalls and rapids are common sites for ghost sightings. This is especially true of the rivers and streams that feed Lake Superior. Such tales often go back to stories first told by the Sioux, Ojibwe, and Menominee. References to such origins can be found in contemporary stories even though the full cultural significance sometimes eludes today's storytellers.

Waterfall ghosts with a hint of American Indian lineage can be found at Brownstone Falls on Tyler Forks, Copper Falls on Bad River,

Morgan Falls on Morgan Creek, and on the Montreal River system at Superior Falls, Saxon Falls, Gile Falls, Rock Cut Falls, and Spring Camp Falls.

It is also common in Wisconsin for overlooks and cliffs to be associated with tales of tragic death for star-crossed lovers. The Wisconsin River cliff ghost near Lone Rock is perhaps the best known of these "long drop" ghosts. The phantom lovers at Big Manitou Falls share one significant feature with the Lone Rock tale: the idea of parallel story versions for both European-Americans and American Indians.

The setting is one of Wisconsin's most scenic state parks. This, I find, is a hindrance to story collection efforts. Despite the many ghost sightings at Aztalan, Blue Mound, Devil's Lake, High Cliff, Roche-A-Cri, Tower Hill, Wildcat Mountain, and Wyalusing, the Department of Natural Resources is extremely reluctant to publicize unusual phenomena. Agency employees are usually tight-lipped. In this case, Casey, a volunteer worker at Pattison State Park, breaks the official silence.

🌿 🌿 🌿

We're not supposed to talk about it. But what are they going to do, fire me? They're already so short of volunteers and they've already cut so many state employee jobs over the years—well, it makes you wonder if the DNR knows what premier attractions its parks are.

Besides, I'll bet more people would come to see the falls if the ghost story was publicized. It's not as if people would start holding seances there at midnight.

From what I hear, these stories of tragic falls for boyfriends and girlfriends are pretty common. But I bet those other places don't have anywhere near the number of sightings that we do here at Pattison State Park. And I'm sure this is the only place where the ghost lovers reenact their jump.

From what I've heard about ghosts it is typical to know a fair amount about their origins, but actual observations are pretty rare. So the focus is usually on the history or folklore and less on the manifestations. Here, it's the reverse. I know of dozens of sightings in recent times. But the background of the ghosts is obscure and contradictory.

About all anybody can be sure of is that there are two ghosts. One male and one female. It's how they came to become ghosts that is hotly disputed. You can't imagine the variations on this story!

What you hear most often is double suicide. That fits in with the forbidden love theme. Then there's the murder-suicide version. So some think it was unrequited love.

We also have the triangle theories. Those include double murder, murder-suicide, double suicide-murder, double murder-suicide, and even triple suicide. But that last option isn't supported by our two ghost sightings.

There's even a theory about them not being ghosts at all. Something about them being creatures from another dimension who use some power in the falls as transportation between levels of existence. That's pretty farfetched pseudoscience if you ask me.

Then there are those who say the whole thing is an optical illusion. And it's true the sightings are linked to certain conditions. That brings us to the ethnic versions. And it's only fair to take the Indian spins on this first.

I'm still trying to find out from the old medicine men what the real traditions are. Not the embellished "my grandmother was a Cherokee princess" stuff. More on the connections to the manitou.

We hear sometimes that it was a forbidden Sioux-Chippewa romance. Sort of an Indian Romeo and Juliet. I don't think that was likely. There are also versions of their intertribal combinations. Most of them don't seem likely because of distance or because the tribes mentioned weren't in conflict. Some see it as an offshoot of the Hiawatha epic. Some even say the lovers are captives of the manitou. Something about the manitou wanting the woman for himself.

Then we have the white "captive" woman versions. It's never something more plausible like mixed-blood woman or French-Canadian woman. Never mind involuntary captivity, which would have left many historical references.

There's the captive Norwegian woman. The captive Irish woman. The captive German woman. Now there's one for the books. Any Indian man who takes a German hostage as a wife will be guaranteed to throw himself over a big waterfall. And hope she doesn't follow.

That feeds into the totally white versions of the story. I've heard it told as a Norwegian, Irish, German, Russian, and Finnish story. And as mixtures between those groups. But I guess in the end, none of that is really important. I mean, what are we going to do, have genetic testing of the ghosts?

If you intend to see the ghosts you have to hit it at the right time. Both on time of day and time of year. The light, the wind, and the temperature has to be just right.

There can be a couple mornings or even a dozen mornings each spring and fall that are just right. But some years you might get none. Like in those years with no spring at all. Most often this time falls in late May and early October. Then you need to be there right at sunrise. Right in those seconds before the first ray of sun hits the top of the falls.

You need a quick temperature change. One that generates a fog layer on the upper Black River. Just so the fog is drifting over the falls like water. It takes a slight south wind. Of course conditions might be perfect and you still may not see them. Maybe it's the angle.

And when you do see them it's very subtle and delicate. These aren't your halloween story ghouls in period costume. No, they appear in two wispy ways. Sometimes they appear as two clear spots in the mist. Other times they appear as well-defined figures made up of mist.

The sequence is that they float down the river on the fog, pause ever so briefly at the top of the falls, and then plunge over. Sometimes it looks like they embrace on the way down. Sometimes it looks like they turn into a rainbow. I think the whole thing is beautiful and pretty benign. Who's harmed by any of this?

Last summer we had one old grouchy guy who passed through and started scaring people. You know the type. Big mouth and loud opinions. He said that the love story was bunk. That it was just a cover for murders. He talked about how the old mound-builders first threw people over as a sacrifice. And about how later on trappers tossed over partners to avoid splitting bounty.

He said a place that gets used in that way develops an appetite for more death. Almost like it needs to be fed. The way he was sputtering and carrying on he may have had some kind of brain problem. But maybe he was a lifelong crank.

He cut quite a figure. I'll never forget him. Wiry in his old age. With a 101st Airborne t-shirt and a D-day commemorative baseball cap. And a leather patch over one eye. He laughed and said how there was whole bunches of people he'd like to feed to those falls.

26

PART II

Lake and Loon Country

The Guardians of Ouija Board Rock

Wisconsin's North Country has become a refuge of sorts for many independent-minded individuals. From the 1960s on, there has been a slow but steady influx of back-to-the-landers, neo-pagans, and redneck hippies. One side effect of this in-migration has been the development of a sturdy, if crabby, brand of rural feminism.

Women migrants were left to tend children and gardens in isolated cabins. Their male partners often worked at distant construction jobs or occupied themselves with hunting and fishing (or else seldom emerged from the clouds of their homegrown Wisco weed).

It is almost impossible to attend a northwoods social event without overhearing women sharing their frustrations about leaky roofs, faulty plumbing, balky woodstoves, and the men who promised to fix those problems. While their hardships breed a certain amount of bitterness, a goodly portion of self-reliance is also evident. It is these women who organize the local peace and environmental groups, staff the charities, and run the co-ops.

As a result there is a certain amount of feminist culture: music, publications, and support groups. Women's storytelling and folklore soon follows. Our source here knows many stories that flow from the experience of northwoods women. But she only knows of one ghost tale. Karen tells it in a Woodland Center cabin made hot by a day of woodstove breadmaking.

🌿 🌿 🌿

Women around here usually don't have time for ghost stories. I've always associated ghost stories with men hanging out at the neighborhood tavern. Or hiding at the hunting shack or at their favorite fishing spot.

So I confess my mental association between ghost stories and the male tendency to disappear during domestic crises. That, plus the age-old male tendency to use the scary story as a way to keep women in their place. That's what most religion is, don't you think? Rules to keep women barefoot and pregnant?

That's different from women's spirituality. Less focus on control. Also we don't have to ponder the Holy Spirit. There are spirits everywhere and they're all holy because in a truly spiritual view everything is sacred.

When my women friends told me about the guardians of Ouija Board Rock I thought it was one of those haunted place stories. But far from it. It was a place for women to get in touch with the spiritual side. I guess these spirits are ghosts in the usual sense. I mean that they had prior human form.

A small group of women who moved out from the Twin Cities twenty years ago have been using it as a meditation spot all these years. They knew it was special right from the start. The place got its name from the rock in the center of the clearing and its special attributes. It was soon discovered that the rock could answer questions. That's why they thought of a ouija board.

It's a flat table-like boulder with rounded stones on top. Stones like you'd find in a stream bed. And they move around in response to inquiries. Well, at least part of the time. At first it was thought to be magnetism or something like that. But a woman shaman from Maine told us about the three spirit guardians.

She said they're old, old spirits. She called them pre-great flood spirits. But she couldn't get a fix on their origins. Some of the women think the spirits are ancient Indian medicine women. Others think that they're priestesses from the goddess times.

I know you've come a long way. But I can't show you the place. The others made me promise I wouldn't. It's not like it's some special women's place unviolated by men. I'm sure hunters have stumbled by it. And from the beer cans left behind we know that it's been used as an under-age drinking hideout.

The others are just afraid of bringing outside attention to it. They think you'll write some travelogue that starts off innocently enough with a casual mention of sights along Wisconsin's magical river road and its Indian trail origin. But they don't want outsiders closer than Highway 35.

The local men know about what we do there. Well, sort of. It's not like there's been a man-woman discussion about it. Yeah, we talk, they barely listen, and then they just sort of grunt. It's that old problem— women are from Venus and men are from way past the Crab Nebula. You mention spirituality and they don't get it. Or every once in awhile one gets it, but doesn't care about it.

The place serves an important function. It's a place to talk things through. A place to bring north country women together to break down our problems of geographic distance and isolation. The spirits there are part of our sisterhood. So I guess we feel some ownership. It's on woman-owned land.

As far as how it works, well, we have a routine. We operate on a lunar cycle. But I can't tell you what phase. And we have our special seasonal ceremonies. Usually it's a dozen or two women. Sometimes close to a hundred. Mostly single parent mothers. But a sprinkling of Wiccans, older housewives, and women who love women.

The spirits help make it our medicine place—our healing place. They give us signs and give us the strength to take care of the others who depend on us. It's true there's a fair amount of questions to the spirits about male transgressions. Like, is he with another woman, when will the support check arrive, and will he remember his son's birthday this year?

The spirits are pretty accurate—when they're in a mood to talk. Sometimes they seem pre-menstrual. So you just try again.

No one ever actually sees the spirits in a physical way. Just the stones moving, mostly. Although many, including me, have felt light touches on our shoulders, pecks on the cheek, or even warm hugs.

It's our way of fighting the blues, getting recharged, and learning to accept the knuckleheads who father our children and occasionally warm our beds. It's also our way of dealing with the disturbances— the things that you just can't put your finger on.

Men can ignore that stuff. They stay sane through ignoring stuff. Whether its dust bunnies, dishes, dirty diapers, or depressed women. I know you're looking for more serious stuff. Cosmic disturbances. Profound insights. Cultural significance. Well, it's just women doing their own thing here.

You're looking for problems. And we just happen to have an answer machine that won't respond to you. Yeah, we've had a few ominous signs. A few intrusive spirits. But you'll have to trust us. We're working on it.

The Ice Fisherman

One of the pleasures of chasing ghost stories is the occasional good-natured ribbing one takes during searches for sites and sources. A total skeptic will give you a disdainful snort. A doubter will often just turn away. And the bubbly over-eager source sometimes has other motivations and needs that invite caution on the part of the story collector.

But when the story collector finds himself or herself the butt of wisecracks and giggling stage whispers, then it is virtually guaranteed that a ghost story will follow. It is almost as if some sources insist on distancing themselves from ghost lore by affecting a light-hearted stance. It may well be that it is also their way of testing aspiring folklorists to assess levels of pretense and academic constipation.

My zigzagging journey across northern Wisconsin had amounted to fairly serious business. Even the stories with humorous components were laden with cultural significance. By the time I pulled over at the Rhinelander Beer sign near Manitowish Waters on Highway 51, I was overdue for a ghost story told with a wink of the eye.

The tavern had a smoke-darkened knotty pine character. The faded signs of long-gone and unavailable brews hung on the walls like memorial plaques: Walters of Eau Claire, Leidiger of Merrill, Farmers of Shawano, Mathie-Ruder of Wausau, Northern of Superior, and, of course, the original Rhinelander. The usual collection of dusty and moth-eaten trophy fish and deer loomed in dark corners. Blue pipe smoke snaked its way the length of the bar. A lazy card game punctuated by grunts held sway at a bottle-laden table.

Altogether, a perfect place for storytelling and story listening. Alas, it's gone now.

It was not given the dignity of demolition or even abandonment. Instead it was rehabilitated. A ghoulish process that left it looking like a surgically assembled collection of disparate body parts and amenities calculated to fill the parking lot with Illinois license plates.

This story, therefore, also serves as a memorial to a once visited place where a now deceased "old duffer" told stories. Avery knew changes were coming and threatened to haunt the place with his laughter and wisecracks.

Ghost stories? You're chasing ghost stories when you could be chasing skirts? You rode a motorcycle without a helmet, right?

So what kind of ghost story guy are you? The Loch Ness Monster and aliens from Mars kind? Or the past lives and talking to your dead Egyptian princess cousin kind?

Well, funny you should ask. It just so happens I know a ghost story. Actually I've heard hundreds of ghost stories from the boozers and losers in here, but I've only ever heard one that I give the benefit of the doubt to. The rest come from eating raw onions at night or from Wild Turkey with Leinenkugel chasers.

I give this one the benefit of the doubt because it was told to me by the cleanest living man in these parts. He didn't drink or smoke and he had low cholesterol. I'd be a total believer if it weren't for the fact that he had bad eyes. He thought his wife—my sister—was beautiful. He thought Hurley was a nice town.

So there you have it. Even a good man has flaws that color his judgment. But he swore by this story. And he was a sincere man. A good church man. Decent father and grandfather. Never cheated so much as a paper boy.

Now this wasn't one of your rooted ghosts. Not stuck in one place like the alleged wailing up on Papoose Creek or rumor of the headless guy down in Powell Marsh. No, the ice fisherman ghost has quite a range. My brother-in-law saw the darn thing on Circle Lily Lake, Dead Pike Lake, Birch Lake, and Big Crooked Lake. Probably some others I forgot.

Now I'm a muskie fisherman myself. I've fished them with live squirrels on wooden shingles for bait. Had to shoot some with thirty-eight caliber revolvers just to get them in the boat. So a ghost icefishing doesn't impress me a whole lot.

I never liked icefishing much. A time or two with the grandkids each winter does it for me. I mean just standing out there in the cold. The Good Lord never intended it. He gave us a brain, right? The way I look at it, these chronic ice fishermen all deserve to come back as ghosts on the ice. Let them all have icicles hanging off their buttocks. Then, for them, hell will have frozen over.

But back to my brother-in-law's ghost story. It had to be one of those died-in-the-wool ice fishermen. The ones whose wives run off with vacuum cleaner salesmen and whose kids can't recognize them.

He's said to be out there all the time from the first solid freeze to when the ice gets mushy. So four or five months a year is common. What's unusual about him is the amount of times he's seen in the day. Often in swirling snow. Sometimes in little snow whirlwinds. Almost white-out conditions.

Of course he's seen in the moonlight and starlight too. He's there and then he's not there. This, I'm told, is the way ghost fishermen operate. They're usually visible only for a short time.

But ghost fishermen are a dime a dozen up here. Only we've got a ghost ice fisherman. With the other ghost fishermen there's usually more of a story. A name, some history, and sometimes an incident like a drowning. Sometimes even a good physical description.

But with the ice fisherman ghost there's nothing like that. No background. Just the ghost in his hooded parka. This simplicity makes me partial to the story. I feel like I can trust that it's not loaded down with things people thought of later.

If you're really on this ghost mission you'll find lots of these outdoorsmen ghosts. Learn to sniff them out. There's always an old guy telling the story, right? But he's usually telling the story about how another old guy told him the story. And the other old guy is always toothless, or missing fingers, or has some deformity.

Watch out for those guys. It's one thing to tell a story that maybe didn't happen and then again maybe it did. It's different for some of these guys. They like to manipulate people. Send them off on missions.

I say don't fool with those old guys. Forget the hints of secrecy and hidden meanings. Find some laughter and a simple message. Like with our ice fisherman ghost. My brother-in-law found him to be a good indicator of where the fish were. Better than a new fishfinder.

It worked for my brother-in-law. He caught lots of fish. And it kept his marriage happy. That's right. He didn't go everyday, all day and then come home without fish. Women distrust that. Heck, he came home early and cleaned the fish too. A stand-up guy!

So stick to the bars where you know you're getting part story and part fully digested cattle food. Stay away from those lonely boat landings at night. But you won't listen, will you?

This tavern will be gone soon. Heck, most of us customers will be gone soon, too. Do me a favor, okey? Come back in a few years and see if it's haunted. If I have my way, the ice fisherman will be here with me and we'll both be haunting those Illinois yuppies in their tight bicycle pants.

Lac Vieux Desert's Canoes

The Apostle Islands may represent Wisconsin's northernmost geographical feature. Yet for many, the Wisconsin River headwaters represent the essence of the northwoods.

There are ghosts to be found the entire length of the Wisconsin River. It is probably the most haunted river in the world. Some say the river itself is a spirit. It is a spirit coursing and pulsing through the heart of Wisconsin. It is a spirit rich with the earthy mystery of all its departed travelers and sojourners.

Many of the Wisconsin River's ghost stories are complex. Some defy explanation even within the assumptions of spirit lore. But it is entirely fitting that the headwaters ghost story flows from the pure and simple north country life.

The storyteller here represents a fading part of the north country scene. He is a Milwaukee lathe operator with Vilas County roots. He maintains a weekend shack on County E, not a lakefront timeshare. He carries a squared-end rowboat on the roof of his beat-up station wagon, not a slick twin-engine job behind a late model four-wheel drive.

He is fond of stories and is easy to draw out. He knows the country between Eagle River and Presque Isle like he knows his backyard. He can be found in baitshops and taverns throughout the region.

On one particular evening he lingered at the boat landing at the southwest end of Lac Vieux Desert. Maxwell was holding court at a circle around a lantern. He updated his listeners on their private story.

🌿 🌿 🌿

Anybody see anything special out there today? It was another day of blinding beauty. Don't ya just wish that you could freeze a day like this and keep it forever?

If ya got an early start ya probably saw that sunrise in the mist. And ya musta heard the loons up by Marsh Bay. My ears told me that the Michigan wardens put in just before dawn. Then they puttered out behind Draper Island's western point. They zipped out about nine a.m. to creel-check a couple of drifting Illinois boats. But I think the suckers came up empty.

And yeah, I saw the canoes in that early mist. This time a line of three with two paddlers apiece. Not a sound as they passed and barely a ripple as they paddled. This time they came out of the channel between Duck Island and Michigan Point. I've seen that before, but it's more common for them to come right out of the marsh on the north end of the lake.

I've seen them now a hundred-fifty, may two hundred times since 1946. Each time there's something a little different about them. The cut of the prow. The smell of hides or dried meat. Pointed paddles or blunt paddles.

Sometimes it's the number of canoes. It goes from one to a dozen or more. And sometimes it's the type of canoe. It can be a line of authentic Chippewa birch barks. Or a couple of restored Old Towns or brand spanking-new Lincolns. A few rare times it was even a mix of old and new.

I saw them the first time with Pop right after he came home from the merchant marine in World War Two. He wrote me many times from the Murmansk run and later from the South Pacific to promise we'd go fishing as soon as he got back. I was only twelve then. But Pop told me it was time for me to learn the things that being a man in my family meant. I guess that meant hunting and fishing mostly.

But at the time it seemed like there was a lot of card playing, greasy cooking, swearing, farting, and storytelling. Pop told me what he knew about the ghosts in canoes. Which wasn't much. Just that people had been seeing ghosts in canoes ever since anybody remembered.

Like all things a father teaches ya, ya later learn that there's more to it. Maybe the father is not a good talker. Maybe the son is not a good listener. Maybe they're just different about what's important.

But over the years I learned there was more to this than ghostly figures on one lake. It's bigger than that. It's got something to do with the whole of northern Wisconsin and the length of the Wisconsin River.

Partly it's through the ghosts themselves. They're a diverse lot. And they represent many things. There's lost war parties, drunken traders, frozen trappers, murdered smugglers, storm-swamped fishermen, and even ditzy tourists. They represent the many ways life can be claimed on the waters. And believe me, there's lots of ways.

It didn't take me long to figure out they weren't all claimed on Lac Vieux Desert. No, there's kind of a hole from this dimension to the spirit world on the upper part of the lake. So there's a big river on the other side of that hole. A river of spirits that runs deep with souls. And that hole somehow leaks out the lost Northwoods souls.

Darn if I know the mechanics of the darn thing. Or if there's any schedule or master plan. I've heard lots of explanations. One lady came looking for her dead husband. She wanted to hold a seance out on Duck Island. Her theory was that you can't take a soul away from the place the person loved until it's ready to go.

A half Chippewa, half Menominee guy told me it's a journey of souls. That they journey out to take care of unfinished business. He felt that when they're free they get to go down the Wisconsin, then the Mississippi and out into the ocean.

Another Indian told me it's a sorting function. Something about each person having a spirit that's water, sky, earth, or fire. And with the add-on of clan ties. So if you're a water person or come from a fish clan you're gonna pass over on Lac Vieux Desert.

There are tribal elders who connect this to the lights at Watersmeet over in the U.P. The old ones know something about this that they're not telling. I heard they talk to those lights and the glow at Land O' Lakes. There's a connection to this spirit hole.

There's all sorts of stories about why this power is located here. But nothing consistent. In one story it is the place of creation. In the next it's the home of the manidogs. In another the site of a battle between Wenebojo and a windigo. So there's all that spirit stuff floating around here.

But after years and years of looking at the ghost side of this I figured out that I was overlooking the obvious. I mean ghosts and stories about ghosts come out of a way of life. And up here we are losing a way of life.

I'm talking about the way things were before. The old north. The north of the old fishing camps. Of two week family vacations with wives playing cribbage and sunburnt and mosquito-bitten kids.

Those were the days before condos and chamber of commerce development plans. Nobody had to worry about builders tearing up the landscape. Nobody thought about Indians and whites fighting over fish that were unsafe for pregnant women and children to eat. That was the northwoods of loon cries and starlight on calm lakes. Before jet skis and casino glare.

But the ghosts helped me see that we can't really go back. Much as we'd like to. The things we really like belong to our slice of time and place. That's why the ghosts keep themselves in the clothes and canoes of their time.

As far as encounters with the ghosts go, there isn't much else to say. Mostly, I've just watched them. As far as I know they never talk to anybody. Just growling from a commonly seen one-eyed ghost.

Their range is impressive, though. I've heard of them going all the way down the Wisconsin. I followed three canoes down as far as the Rainbow Flowage. I've seen them on Willow Reservoir and on Lake Lucerne. I've heard pretty reliable reports about them running the Wolf River and making the Wisconsin to Fox portage.

I'll be retiring soon. Then I'm moving back up here permanently. Maybe add on to the shack for guests. Get some decent plumbing in there.

Then I plan to follow those canoes as much as I can. Not to make a spectacle of them like them kids who drove the boat through the ghosts—and wrecked their boat. No, I just want to find the place the canoes come out of. Maybe I'll figure out a way to get on the other side of that hole. I'd like to check it out over there.

Peeksville's Naked Ghosts

Wisconsin Finns occupy a strange niche in our ethnic folklore. They are not always thought of as the Northern Europeans they are. Instead, they seem to be thought of as more exotic and somehow set apart.

The old New Englander stock who owned the businesses and ran the courts in the early days found the Finns to be subversive, profane, and violent. Their two-fisted exuberance on behalf of labor unions and other social activist causes was viewed with alarm.

Finnish-American themes and characters pop up in many northwoods stories. They are especially evident in lumberjack and iron miner ghost tales. These robust Finnish-American ghost stories are abundant in Minnesota's Iron Range, Michigan's Upper Peninsula, and in Iron, Ashland, and Douglas counties in Wisconsin.

The stories are usually told by purebred Finns possessed of fierce pride in their heritage.

Further south the bloodlines and stories peter out. Those of partial Finn blood are often ambivalent about Finnish-American folklore and sometimes are totally ignorant about it.

The following story made its way into this collection because it was the southernmost Finnish ghost story that retained its full ethnic flavor. It also merited inclusion because its theme was so different from the typical Finnish hero ghost.

Finally, it was unique in that its source maintained a multi-ethnic perspective. Alexander confessed surprise at outside interest in the tale.

🔥 🔥 🔥

No one has asked about the Peeksville Ghosts in a long time. You don't hear the old Finnish stories around here anymore. Not like you still can in Hurley and Ashland.

The really old Finns are gone now. My grandsons and granddaughters never met any of the genuine oldtimers. And the Finn part of our family is thinning out. I'm only a quarter Finn so the grandchildren are only one sixteenth. Not much for them to hook up with when hardly any of their friends have any Finn blood either.

But in a way these Finnish ghosts in Peeksville had as much to do with the other groups around here. At least with how the other groups saw the Finns. In addition to my quarter Finn blood, I'm a quarter French. That's about as Wisconsin as you can get. All I'd need is a dash of Chippewa, and who knows, maybe that's in the French part.

All sides of the family were connected to the railroad. They hailed from places like Park Falls, Mellen, and Butternut. The ghost story was connected to railroading in a way. At least it was in the old days.

In the old days the ladies didn't like to talk about it because, you see, the ghosts were naked. Yah, naked as newborn babes. People started seeing those naked ghosts right around World War One. They saw them from on the train. There was a combination train of boxcars, log flatcars, and a passenger coach that ran from Ashland to Park Falls. I think it was a morning and evening run.

Well, it just so happened that the train was in the vicinity of Peeksville at dawn and dusk. There were other passenger trains in those days—the line ran from Ashland to Wisconsin Rapids—but they were pretty much midday runs. On that old combination train they would see the naked Finns running through the weeds in the twilight. They was always headed east toward Schraum Creek. To dive in and cool off I guess. That was a key part of the story. These naked Finns were coming out of a hidden sauna somewhere.

Now my French grandmother said the sauna was in hell itself. She always claimed a Finn could barely work up a sweat down there. And she was married to one. My German grandfather thought the sauna custom was barbaric. But his Norwegian wife thought it was a fine thing to do as long as you maintained your modesty with a towel or at least stuck to same sex groups.

It was the mixed naked men and women that bothered a lot of people. I never understood that. I mean they're ghosts, they're dead. As long as you're seeing a moldy old ghost, what's the difference whether they're dressed or not? Isn't the whole point of a ghost to goose our souls and our brains?

I think that it offended many people that these naked ghosts were old and decrepit like me. There was a lot of belly flab, big rear ends, wrinkles, and sagging stuff to see. More people would have looked forward to it if the ghosts had been in the prime of life. Then a naked body is a work of art.

Now some said that what you saw depended on who you were. I mean, as far as family background. Norwegians supposedly saw normal-looking people. French saw wild lust-driven creatures. Germans saw hideous beings. And Finns saw beautiful maidens and handsome young bucks. The rest of us crossbreeds just saw old bags and old farts. At least that's what I saw.

These ethnic group ways of seeing things made a great deal of difference back then. Before the groups intermarried it really influenced your life. It really worked out that way on railroad jobs. The Germans were engineers and brakemen up here. The Norwegians worked on the track and bridge crews. The French were the freight clerks and conductors. The Finns had the dirty jobs of engine oilmen and freight carmen.

Now supposedly this was another thing that connected to the naked Finns. There was a lot of misunderstanding about Finnish hygiene because they often had dirty jobs. Add that to their preference for the sauna over the bath and you create a bad impression.

There was all sorts of ritual around Finnish use of the sauna. It was a religious experience. There was a quiet time and a social time. And special sauna rituals on certain days. Every Finn had to take a

Shrove Tuesday sauna for good luck. They got clean in there too. They scrubbed themselves with rough pads and sponged off. But people still thought the Finns were dirty.

So that was part of the prejudice against the ghosts too. What could be nastier than a bunch of old ugly and dirty ghosts? They're not seen as much as they once were. Of course, there's not much travel on those tracks anymore except for the new short-line freights. So every once in a while a train crewman will see the naked ghosts. Or sometimes some kids will get scared by them.

It's been years since I last saw them. But then since I moved away from the family homestead and up here to Glidden, I just don't get to walk down around Schraum Creek anymore.

But, you never know, a couple of us senior citizens might inspire the ghosts again. An old friend just built a sauna out of an old steam locomotive boiler up on Meyers Lake Road. And he knows two Finnish sisters our age from up in High Bridge who are raring to get their clothes off.

The Sioux Warriors of Strawberry Island

Wisconsin is blessed with a number of places that have over-lapping layers of legend and lore. Prairie du Chien, Green Bay, and Madeline Island spring immediately to mind. The layers are usually connected to successive waves of settlement or to shifting political con-trol (...Indian, French, British, American). Thus, the long-settled fort and trading post sites have the most evidence of these layers.

Rural and isolated sites are less likely to exhibit this story-stacking phenomena. In these less-traveled places story continuity is often broken. Neglect is also compounded where the stories are American Indian and the setting is a reservation.

The Lac du Flambeau Indian Reservation offers a site that is rich in its antiquity and its legends. There, on Strawberry Island, we find *a location with a thousand years of ghosts to account for. Sorting them out is the problem.*

Wendell, a Lac du Flambeau construction worker, offered to help sift through the stories on his lunch break at a Bolton Lake construction site. He excavated these comments in a straightforward backhoe style.

🌾 🌾 🌾

We were always told that Strawberry Island was home to a lot of ghosts. Sometimes we called it "ghost island." Some called it "bone island." It was even called "poison ivy island," although the poison ivy was blamed on spirits too.

Now I can tell you stories from out there on the island. But if you want to know the meaning of things out there you must ask a medicine man. I approach these things respectfully even though I don't understand them all. All my generation can do is try to remember what the grandfathers, grandmothers, and old Canadian relatives said.

The main story is about the battle with the Sioux and the tremendous slaughter there. But there are much older stories that are hazy on details. In our old stories there are the four famous sons of Winona, fathered by the Great Spirit. Three of the sons are remembered for the gifts they brought to the Ojibwe. But the second son, Pukawiss, is almost forgotten.

Pukawiss was viewed by some as a no-account and vagabond. He traveled and entertained and danced. So you might say he was the original powwow bum. Pukawiss never had a permanent home. And when he died his spirit could not be confined to one place. But in life he had used Strawberry Island as a resting place and that is where his ghost now goes in between haunting today's pow-wows.

Some stories connect Strawberry Island to the great epic story of the Ojibwe. How the Anishinabe people were told by a prophet to leave their home on the Atlantic Ocean and travel west to look for food that grows on water. In other words, wild rice. Lac du Flambeau was in this area where food grew on water. But the area was already occupied by the Sioux. And Strawberry Island was important to them.

The island was an important place for visions. They and the Winnebago had used the place for thousands of years for burials. Misunderstandings about use of the island and the rice in surrounding

42

waters set off conflict. Soon it was a full-scale war for control of the wild rice country.

This war raged from the Upper Peninsula to the St. Croix area. But it all came to a head with the battle on Strawberry Island about three hundred years ago. It was a battle in which thousands fought and hundreds died. In the end the Sioux were defeated and driven from wild rice country. Their dead warriors and the bones of their ancestors were abandoned.

Some say this abandonment led to the severe haunting of Strawberry Island. That there are hundreds of lonely and angry ghosts out there. I've only ever met one person who saw ghosts out there—it's not a place we go a lot. He saw a group with painted faces and bloody war clubs.

But I and many others have often heard the ghosts. During late summer the shouts, whoops, and screams can be heard toward evening. The Sioux warriors. Some say it is the noise and pain of the Sioux casualties. But others say that it is the dead of both sides reenacting the battle.

All in all, it is a place to be avoided or at least approached carefully because of the unsettled spirits of the Sioux warriors. Yet there is even more reason to be cautious. When the French came, the missionaries took note of the island as a sacred place. They tried to plant a cross out there. A bear killed a missionary. So there's a priest ghost out there too.

Then the U.S. Indian agents got the idea that there were graves and treasures to rob out there. They sent some flunkies out to dig the stuff up. They never came back. That meant some more ghosts on the island.

Later, during Prohibition, we often had the gangsters come up here. They hid Canadian whiskey on the reservation. They took a squealer out to the island to kill him. A fight broke out and three or four killed each other. More ghosts.

Finally, we have the development stuff. You know that we lost ownership of the island through that corrupt Dawes Allotment Act? That law should have been called the "shove-a-deed-in-front-of-an-Indian-and-make-him-sign-it-quick-act."

But we now have the battle over whether white developers will put a resort on top of two-thousand-year-old burial sites. Then there's the question about what the tribal government will do. What will the medicine men do? What will the Sioux do? What will the State Historical Society do?

In a normal place the answers would be easy. But with Vilas County in the picture and the boatlanding riots and look-the-other-way law enforcement in mind, it should prove very interesting.

This may become the first haunted site ever that gets written up by political reporters. Before it's done we could have the American Indian Movement, the skinheads, the environmentalists, and those corporate land rapers up here. Who knows, maybe a new battle and some new ghosts?

All I know is that I would not want to operate a piece of heavy equipment on Strawberry Island. I wouldn't want to use a chainsaw out there. I have a hunch that it will be an accident-prone place. If something were ever to be built out there, well, nothing good would come from it. Let's just say you wouldn't want your family staying there.

I wouldn't want to be responsible for the falls, drownings, stabbings, and shootings that will occur out there once those Sioux warriors can take over a live body. But that's nothing to some Chicago suit out to make a buck.

The Phantom Snowmobiler

Wisconsin's archetypal outdoors ghosts count many a fisherman, hunter, and logger among their number. Most of the stories have deep roots or at least established traditions to draw upon. Even outdoor ghosts of relatively recent origin can be analyzed within the framework of familiar settings like the fishing camp or the hunting shack. The feel of flannel, the scent of pine, and call of the loon are as much a part of such stories as the usual haunted place features.

Deep winter settings produce fewer tales unless there is a connection to winter madness or cabin fever. Fewer still have a thoroughly outdoor winter setting (The Ice Fisherman is an exception). It may also say something about ghosts and the tellers of ghost stories that even most noisy ghosts are disconnected from the sounds of machinery.

There is not much evidence of ghost linkage to power boats, jet skis, and all-terrain vehicles.

This makes the Woodruff tale of the Phantom Snowmobiler all the more surprising. Like the motorcyclist ghost of Ridgeway (Driftless Spirits, Prairie Oak Press, 1996), there is an unmistakable anti-traditional element to the story.

The narrator personifies the Wisconsinites who rarely get to tell their stories and feel alienated because no one listens. He is a large man. He sweats profusely in the summer heat even as we sit directly in the path of the tavern fan. He longs for winter. He lives for winter.

His Marine Corps bicep tattoos jump as he clenches fists in emphasis of his points. He explains that he really did not want to hurt the TV weatherman who he threatened after a forecast of snow fell through. Dale seems to be like a man who is not afraid of anything. At least until you get him on the right subject.

🔥 🔥 🔥

I didn't believe in ghosts before. I probably still wouldn't give a crap if I hadn't run into the one we got up here. They call him the Phantom Snowmobiler. I called him a nut-cutting son-of-buck.

They started talking about him about ten years ago. Back then people saw him running late on Highway J out toward Pickerel Lake. I remember thinking that the taverns were using cheap stuff in those Korbel bottles. I saw funny things once on cheap tequila.

But then about two years later I saw it myself. A bunch of us were on Woodruff Road south of Hemlock Lake. An old clunker Arctic Cat pulled out of the gravel pit road—almost wiped me out. It was the most beat-up piece of crap I'd ever seen.

But when I tried to catch it he left me eating snow. He must have hit a hundred miles per hour when he got on the straightaway of Highway 47. Then he doubled back on Mid Lake Road. When we made the beer and pee break down at Lake Tomahawk, the others told me it was the ghost. I told them that no dead treadjumper was going to get the better of me.

So I set about trying to catch him. Saw him two or three times a winter for about five years. Chased him all the way to McNaughton one time. He ran me off the trail twice, dumped me off a bridge once, and led me onto thin ice on Minocqua Lake. He made it across. I didn't.

45

I was fit to be tied. I wanted a piece of him in the worst way. I even thought about mounting assault rifles on my tread job. Silly, huh?

Well, I mellowed a little. A big guy like me can work up a belly full of hate that will kill him. You get ticked off, you get that grease and booze cooking in your gut, you get that cigarette smoke boiling in your brain, and the next thing you know you're working on ulcers, high blood pressure, blood clots in the head, and popping hemorrhoids. That's when a guy will knock around the wife and the kids. So it's good that mine left long ago.

But one of my good semper fi buddies from the Corps told me I had to learn to accept things I can't change. And just to make sure I learned the lesson he cold-cocked me good with a beer bottle the next time he caught me after a highspeed ghost chase.

Then a funny thing happened. I stopped chasing the ghost and he starting finding me. Yeah, riding just ahead of me. Sometimes alongside of me. This is when I started getting a good look at him. I think I'm about the only one who's spent that much time close to him.

Others have described his old Arctic Cat snowmasher. And I can vouch for its crappy looks. But I'd swear that thing could leave Woodruff and make the North Pole in thirty-six hours. The ghost himself is a throw-back. No fancy clothes or boots. No shiny helmets. He's wearing a set of greasy gray insulated coveralls. A G.I. earflapped hat on his head. Buckle overshoes on his feet.

But when you get up close you notice something startling real quick. You look at his face and there is none! Yeah, just a blank space under the visor of the hat. So there's no talk and no eyes to give you signals. About all I could ever figure from him was from his hands. Sometimes he'd point. Sometimes he'd wave. And sometimes he'd stick up his mitten thumb.

His old snowbeater has an odd sound for a snowmobile that age. You know the new ones have high-pitched whines. The old ones sounded like big chainsaws sawing railroad ties. But the ghost's snowbanger just has kind of a hum. Almost like it's running on electric.

So I guess if you keep your pie-hole shut and watch and listen you can learn something. Not that the mucky-mucks and butt-wipes up here would want you to know. No, they don't want the story told. Don't scare the tourists. Don't you know it's bad for the bar and resort business?

But I know that if you follow the patterns you can find omens. The ghost has blocked trails and those who went around him later

46

found themselves through the ice. He tried to run some drunk punks off Highway 47 to save them. But one of those fools gave an electric pole a sixty-mile-per-hour kiss. So I know he's trying to tell us to tone it down. But that's not part of the official plan around here.

I like to wail on my machine as much as the next guy. And I've been known to fuel myself on a bottle of brandy and a twelve-pack so that by bar time I'm twice the legal limit. But I know the trails and I know what I'm doing. What we're getting up here now is a lot of Milwaukee and Chicago rum-dumbs that can barely find their way up here.

Then they get on high-performance machines that they get no practice driving. Then they drink double what they can handle. They go in the night to places they have no experience with. And they think the whole northwoods is an open park.

The ideas of guide wires, private lane cable gates, and barbed wire fences are totally beyond their brain capacity. They're surprised when they're decapitated or have their skulls bashed in. They're shocked when they trespass and cross private land and end up cracked up in somebody's foundation hole.

I think the ghost is trying to stop it. But maybe all those other dead snow jockies left ghosts that are working against him. We better help him or there'll be a snowmobile ghost at every intersection from Stevens Point on up.

The Soldiers' Council

Soldier ghosts are widespread in American folklore. Reports on such ghosts start with the French and Indian War and continue up to today. Wisconsin is home to a number of military ghosts stemming from the War of 1812, the Black Hawk War, and the Civil War. We also know from the Sioux warriors of Strawberry Island that battles in Wisconsin left ghostly casualties.

The warrior, the soldier, and the veteran all occupy an unusual niche in American Indian culture. There is a sense of dignity and honor that seems unconnected to nationalism and politics. Visitors to

47

powwows soon discover that powwow grand entries are led by veterans, that there are special veteran songs and dances, and that only veterans can recover fallen eagle feathers.

In a way it is not surprising that an American Indian soldier's ghost story would be told at a powwow. It is even less surprising that it would be told at a Lac Courte Oreilles powwow. "LCO" is viewed by many Ojibwe as the current center of Anishinabe culture.

The setting is the center drum arbor on the powwow grounds. It is morning and the air is laced with the smells of coffee and fry bread. A small group is gathered to listen to an Ojibwe World War Two veteran. He talks generally of the soldier's proper role in a community. Then Leman surprises them with a ghost story and a prophecy.

🌿 🌿 🌿

Our warriors of the past are still with us. Our passed away veterans seem drawn to this powwow ground. I've known that for years and heard the older veterans—the World War One fellows—talk about things like that. They recalled that the old warrior ghosts were right there with them in the trenches in France.

The old fellows called these ghost gatherings the soldiers' council. The ghost veterans would try to lend their expertise to their descendants. This council is made up of our best fighters. And I don't just mean from here at LCO. I mean from all Anishinabe. From the Canadian tribes, the Three Fires, and the Cree and the Cheyenne.

They are veterans of all the wars. The ancient ones and the modern ones. From the earliest warriors fighting the windigos, to the door-gunners on helicopters. The council even includes Mudjik'wiss, the first son of our people. Son of Winona and Grandson of Nokomis. Mudjik'wiss was our first warrior, the first of our people to make sure that the villages were kept safe.

You must seek direction from the old ones like Mudjik'wiss if you want to understand what it is to be an Ojibwe man. There is more to this than war and fighting. It is about respect. Respect for the earth, for your people, for your leaders, and for your comrades.

When I have been allowed to listen in the soldiers' council in a vision or a dream or when their ghosts have come here, I learn that the warrior's greatest task is to learn how to seek peace. These spirits tell me that there is much honor in protecting and serving our people.

But their wisdom also tells us that much fighting comes from pride and vanity.

These spirits are powerful here in this place. But you can call on them anywhere. Call them in prayer. Offer tobacco. Or hold your eagle feather. You can seek their counsel to help with the questions you face as men. We Anishinabe and other native people have ways to help our veterans and our soldiers. To help them heal and make them whole. The Europeans and others don't.

The warrior spirits tell us that war is an imbalance in the creation. It is not what the Creator wants. So no matter how just the cause or how much honor is found in protecting the people, there is a need to bring the warrior back to harmony and balance.

When a war is done there are dead and disabled. There are widows and fatherless children. There are insane people and drunks and drug addicts. Sometimes even the earth itself is wounded.

I have learned from these warrior spirits in this soldiers' council that the Anishinabe people were given by the Creator the main things we need to help bring back harmony and balance. We have the medicine lodge, the pipe, and the drum. The stories of our people tell us how these gifts of the Creator were given to us. But the warrior spirits can tell you how to use these gifts for strength, healing, and wisdom-seeking.

When you go into the sweat lodge, go with a pure heart. Ask the lodge conductor to help you with your prayers. Let him know what questions you seek answers to or what kind of help you need. In this way you may come to see the warrior spirits yourself or someone else in the lodge may see them for you. You can use tobacco and the pipe to draw on the warrior spirits' knowledge. Many of the pipe carriers are veterans who are on the right path. Remember that the rising smoke carries the prayers up.

The drum is used sacredly to ask permission for things. You can ask the warrior spirits for things this way too. The drums also are used to honor veterans. They are used for the dances that show the continued strength of the Anishinabe.

When I see these warrior spirits in their soldiers' council it is not a scary thing. They sit in a circle as equals. They wear their best ceremonial clothes. Most of them have many eagle feathers. Many are from long ago. Some like Mudjik'wiss are from the beginning of our people. These spirits are here for us. To help us learn to protect the people and protect the earth. Draw on their strength. Draw on their wisdom.

Bad times are coming. Our people will need wise and strong leaders when they come. Families will need strong husbands and fathers. Strong, but wise and loving, too. In the bad times there will be a rising of evil spirits to help the evil living people. The evil spirits will come to push greed, disrespect for the Creator, and hatred of the people who love the Earth.

There will be a final battle of good and evil. The evil spirits and the living evil people will fight the good spirits and the good living people. It will be a very dangerous time and it will test us and all earth-loving people like never before. It may not be exactly like a war. It may be something else, something worse.

But if we make it through, there'll be a good world to live in. A cleansed world like the Creator made in the first place. I know these things from the warrior spirits. A-ho. It is good that you listen to them. Meeg-witch.[3]

The Yellow River Hunter

*Ghosts of hunters are so numerous in Wisconsin as to barely merit attention. My own farm in Iowa County is home to one. (*Driftless Spirits: Ghosts of Southwest Wisconsin, Bethlehem Road Ghosts*). Such tales span the distance from Hazel Green to Lake Superior.*

While there are many recurrent themes in such stories, there are also considerable variations of character and context. It is a bit different with ghost fishermen where the circumstances sometimes indicate that there are not dozens of such ghosts but perhaps only one or two, seen in many spots throughout a region.

Ghosts of hunters seem to run the range of spirit types: phantoms, specters, apparitions, ghouls, and watchers. They can be quaint or

---

[3]Thank you in Ojibwe.

horrible, benign or troublesome. They also often have a clear ethnic identity. German, Norwegian, and American Indian ghost hunters are the most common variations.

The typical hunter ghost story revolves around long sought-after trophy animals. The stories usually focus on the mechanics of the hunt and the technique and skill of the hunter. There is a common theme of ghost intervention. Often there is a surprise ending where the ghost has shape-shifting ability and is able to take the form of the trophy animal.

This ghost story is markedly different. The ghost here falls more into that farm country "helpful" or "chore" ghost category often seen in southern Wisconsin. He is a ghost with a much clearer personal history than the usually enigmatic hunter ghosts.

Up to now it has been a closely held secret in an old Spooner family. Let Big Red, a long haul truck driver, break the silence.

⚜ ⚜ ⚜

This has not been told outside our family. This is our ghost. He's from our family. And if anyone else has seen him—and I think they have—they sure didn't know what to make of him.

We know exactly where he came from and how he got here. He's my great-grandfather's brother. My older relatives always called him "Uncle Frank." But my brothers and I always called him the "Yellow River Hunter."

Doesn't that sound better than "Uncle Frank?" A little more mystery, dignity, and romance?

The Yellow River played a big part in our family's history. They were pioneers up here. First, in the big logging cut and then in the hard-luck, stump-farming homesteading life. Hard times but a good way of life.

Our family story really isn't much different than those of other pioneer families. Few youngsters understand that what they see in their families today represents the survivors. In other words, that part of the family that survived smallpox, cholera, influenza, the Civil War and logging accidents.

Our relative got himself out of the mainstream and got himself into trouble when his first wife died and he took an Indian wife. Actually the second wife had been the hired girl to help the first wife.

51

This put him on the outs with the family and the others around here. But he stuck to himself, raised his family, cleared his stumps, and took pleasure in hunting the Yellow River Country from here all the way over to the St. Croix. He just missed being able to hunt with his brothers and nephews.

Tragedy struck when his second wife had trouble in childbirth. No one would come to help. He probably would have gotten more response if his cow had the same problem. So the Indian wife and the baby died. Then some disease came into the house. Diphtheria, typhoid, something. That took his three children from the first wife.

What happened next is a little unclear. Was he possessed by the same evil thing that brought tragedy to his home? Did he gradually go insane? Or did he just up and kill himself? It's hard to answer those questions after all the time that has passed. We just know that my great-grandfather found his brother's body in the woods with the brother's favorite hunting rifle. An apparent suicide, as they say.

It wasn't a year before the hunters in the family started to see his ghost while hunting. It was always in a friendly sort of way. A wave of the hand or a tip of the hat from a little way off.

Now in our family they grew up on a mixture of English, Scottish, and German ghost stories. So they were surprised when the ghost gave them no trouble. And they had heard of the other hunter ghosts in the area. The one-armed ghost up by Springbrook. The boy hunter ghost at Shell Lake. The old Indian hunter ghost over by Mercer. All of them spooky and on the annoying side.

But our ghost wasn't like that at all. He clearly wanted to be part of the family again. Before long he was not only greeting his brothers and nephews in the woods, he was helping on the hunt. Pushing deer out of the swamps. Flushing out partridges and snowshoe hares.

So it came to be that our family became known as hunters. When others couldn't find game in the entire Yellow River country, our meat-pole was bending under the weight of the fattest does and the biggest bucks. Our Yellow River Hunter has strong ethics too. He's a true sportsman. He helped us shut down a bunch of meat-market poachers. And he's flushed out a couple of local violators so that the warden caught them.

As we all get older this is changing. You don't see the really big deer drives like you once did. Of course, it's not as hard to get a deer as it was forty years ago. So now the Yellow River Hunter just takes up a stand with me or one of the other old-timers.

What's our ghost going to do in the future? Twenty, thirty years ago it looked like each generation would produce more hunters than the ones before it. Now, it's going the other way. I have twelve grandchildren and only two hunt. And one of those is a girl. Both of my daughters have been divorced twice. My son travels on the job so he doesn't have time for his kids. The boys only think about hockey, basketball, and computer games.

When I told my youngest grandson that our family has always hunted with a ghost he looked at me kind of funny. Then he said, "Yeah, right, Grandpa, it's one of those Easter Bunny deals, isn't it?"

Maybe when there are no hunters left in the family then the Yellow River Hunter can rest. Maybe that's what he wants anyway. Maybe he's just been helping and protecting this family until it doesn't need him anymore.

The Lost Spirits of Big Sand Lake

The St. Croix Chippewa do not possess a large land base like many of their brethren of the other Wisconsin Ojibwe reservations. Their land holdings are fragmented like that of the Ho Chunk to the south. Many of the tribe's members feel fortunate that they fought their way back from the official U.S. policy to extinguish the smaller tribes. Their struggle to maintain their identity involved a number of political and cultural features.

This story seems to relate closely to that struggle. It is filled with a sense of what was almost lost and what has yet to be fully regained.

As with many of the stories I heard in reservation country, it draws upon traditional tribal stories and yet puts them in a context of current issues and concerns. Like many of those other stories, it poses the task of sorting out the rich earth-based spirit tradition of the American Indians from the condemned and trapped elements of European-American ghost traditions.

The setting is a campfire near Hertel. A mixed group of Ojibwe, woods hippies, local rednecks, and urban environmentalists debrief from a land-use battle.

The source is a younger man actively exploring his St. Croix Ojibwe roots. He divides his time between a modern apartment in the Twin Cities and a leaky mobile home near Siren. Vic lays it out in reverent tones when he is asked how to win the battle for hearts and minds.

🌿 🌿 🌿

We won't be able to set things straight until we deal with the past. There are restless spirits all across this country which must be put to rest. Spirits at Bad Axe, Wounded Knee, and Fallen Timbers. Spirits of the Pequot, Kickapoo, and Susquehannocks.

I have had to make a lot of my spiritual journey by myself. Some things others can teach you. But much of what's important you must come to know on your own terms and in your own time. I guess I was kind of a lost son. Like my people, I almost lost touch with my past and my heritage. But getting back here—at least part of the time—has helped me reconnect. I've found the sacredness in all things.

It's the three ghosts I've seen that have helped me see this sacredness to life. I saw them when I first started coming back here. I saw the first one in between Lost Lake and Big Sand Lake. It was the ghost of an old man with a drum. And because I was ignorant of ghosts and drums, I had to ask lots of questions and read quite a bit.

As best as I can determine, this ghost is from the time when our people almost fell away from the old ways. He's from a time when he had to search for the scattered people and call them back to the drum. He is the Spirit of the Drum. The drum is sacred because it is the heartbeat. The rhythm of all life. The prayers and songs and dances are the blood that is pumped out through the people and the land to keep us alive. All the original peoples knew the power of the drum. All over the world. But they lost it. We almost lost it. But this ghost reminded me.

The second ghost I saw was another old man. Like the first one, he seemed lost or not sure of where he was. This second ghost I saw along Sand Creek. He was sitting in a clearing and smoking his pipe. The smoke smelled very bitter. Not really like tobacco. I watched him a long time. He did a ceremony which I didn't understand. So I had to ask more questions and study more.

The old Canadian Anishinabe say the pipe was a gift from the fourth and last son born to the Great Mother Winona, daughter of Nokomis. It is said that Winona died in childbirth with the last child. This last son seemed to be everything the people admired. He was strong, smart, and had a sense of humor. And despite his half-spirit birth, he was human in the way of outsmarting himself from time to time. He was called Nahnay-boozoo in old times.

It was this Nahnay-boozoo who was credited with bringing the pipe to the Anishinabe. He brought it back from his spirit father who lived among the manitous. The pipe was to be used as a tool of reconciliation. To be smoked before important undertakings, to offer prayers, and to seal peace.

The pipe was a timely gift because the Anishinabe were falling away from the teachings of the Great Medicine Lodge, what is called the Midewin Society today. The lodge and its clan system brought peace and stability. During this time when the lodge was not followed, factions developed. Men started painting their faces and forming warrior societies. The best hunters turned away from feeding the people and put their energies into war. The people suffered.

Nahnay-boozoo brought the pipe back to the people. He showed them the sacred ways to make pipe bowls and stems. He showed them how to offer prayers with the pipe. There was peace for a long time. I saw this spirit, or the pipe, several times before I heard him say anything I could understand. Before he had mumbled something in old Anishinabe. But suddenly I could understand him.

He was praying and here is what he prayed. He first said, "thank you for the rich earth and our people." Then he went on to pray for the people to be brought back to the pipe. He prayed as if the answer to his prayers could restore him to life. So he obviously thought the power of the pipe could bring him back among the people and restore his youth.

I asked questions about this Nahnay-boozoo of the old people I could find here in Wisconsin. They told me that here he is called Wahnay-boozoo. That he is a trickster who went off from the people because of their failing to follow the sacred teachings. They said that he died of a broken heart and will haunt us until our people are on the right path.

So from this second ghost I learned there is a thin line between guardian angel and fallen angel. And I learned that you must be careful when you use the power of the spirit world. Just as it can be used for good, it can be used carelessly or for evil.

It was awhile before I saw the third ghost. Another old man. This time looking not only lost, but like he lost something, too. I saw this ghost at night near that little opening off Reservation Road where they have the fire pit. I watched him most of the night. He could barely walk and was stumbling off into the dark and returning with sticks. He kept mumbling, too. He was mumbling the instructions for building a sweat lodge.

When I asked questions about this ghost, I determined he was the spirit of an old Midewiwin priest. I learned that a young boy brought the gift of the sweat lodge to the people as the result of his vision quest. The sweat lodge was meant to help the vision quest by purifying the mind and body.

But the sweat lodge had to be done in a very special way. A sacred way. Not only must it be built in a special way, it must be used in a special way. The instructions on how to build it are very clear. First, you offer tobacco before gathering any material. Then you gather willow saplings to make a frame. The frame must have four doors. Only one of those is left open for people. The other three are for spirits.

The east door is the door used by people. The east door faces the outside fire pit where the rocks are heated. The frame is strengthened by four horizontal ring braces that represent the four levels of spiritual knowledge. Everything is lashed together with the inner bark of basswood. You must offer tobacco to find the special rocks that can withstand heat, take the cold water, and send up steam without cracking. Women cleanse the site and place cedar on the path between the fire and the door.

Inside, the doorman sits just to the right of the door. He controls the door and receives the hot rocks. The fireman outside tends the fire, brings the rocks, and trains the apprentices. Four rocks come inside for the Four Directions. Then three more come in to make seven to remind us of the Seven Grandfathers—the seven spirits who taught the boy the ways of the sweat lodge in his vision.

After that, the lodge keeper or conductor handles everything. I don't know that part yet. But it is said that a truly strong conductor can take the lodge out of the physical world and into the spirit world. If he is not careful he will be unable to come back.

There is that whole question of how the sweat lodge is used. There are the rip-offs and the New Age crap. There are Cherokee princesses and con-men who say they were Apache medicine men in past lives. The sweat lodge must be approached with the right outlook. It cannot be a form of recreation or used as a twelve-step program. It is sacred in the deepest sense.

If you want a steambath, use a sauna. Don't make a ramshackle tepee and make up some mumbo-jumbo prayers. Don't pay a couple of hundred bucks to a phony medicine man with a Brooklyn accent. If you're not Indian, wait to be asked. You have your ways to deal with spirits. We have our ways. If you're supposed to end up in the sweat lodge, you will. Don't push it.

The Spirit of the Sweat Lodge helped me learn the lesson that to enter the lodge is to enter the womb of Mother Earth. He helped me learn that the spirits of our ancestors are with us in this life to help us. They are especially present in the lodge.

After my first sweat I came to understand that my third ghost—the Spirit of the Sweat Lodge—is the spirit of that boy from long ago who became the first Midewiwin priest. He comes to pull the scattered people together to make things right again. As time goes on, I see the three spirits together more and more. They look a little less lost. But I know that's because I'm a little less lost.

So what does this all mean to a mixed bunch like this? Well, it means that one of us finds personal significance in these ghosts. I pull meaning out of them. But it means something for everyone in terms of healing and setting right the old wrongs and getting to where we're supposed to be.

There are the ghosts that are trapped in a purgatory. There are evil spirits, too. There are the spirits that are there to help us. We need to encourage each other to build the new culture that draws upon those positive spirits. Once you find the sacredness in everything you can put restless ghosts at peace and hold evil back. I found that in the strangest way. I found sacredness in spearing fish.

Don't laugh. I know that you wouldn't look at the racist yahoos at the boat landings, the slippery politicians, some of the weak-willed tribal officials, and the accompanying media circus and think of spiritual development. But it did work that way for some of us.

Many of the spearing nights were quiet, with no protesters. There were starry nights with the grandfathers staring down on us. There were stormy nights with the manitous buzzing around us. The connection with the ancestors was strong.

You learn to ask the walleye to give up its life to feed the grandmothers and the children. You pray that the boat be filled with the catch.

And you give thanks to the Creator, to the lakes, and to the walleye when the night is done.

I knew spearing was a big part of where I needed to go when I saw my three ghosts this past spring. There they were; the Spirit of the Drum, the Spirit of the Pipe, and the Spirit of the Sweat Lodge. All in a traditional canoe with a torch.

I said nothing since I think of them as my personal ghosts. But they were with us all night. When we got back to the landing, my uncle asked, "Did you notice those ghosts in the canoe tonight?" When I nodded yes, Uncle George smiled, "Good sign, eh?"

Three Lake's Cooler Ghost

The late George Vukelich immortalized Three Lakes, Wisconsin, in his North Country Notebook. *George allowed us to listen in on many conversations at the American Legion bar among his friends: the priest, the doctor, the bartender, and, occasionally, the big Indian. Those conversations were pure northern Wisconsin. Yet, as the participants explored the issues of the day, those conversations also represented every discussion on planet Earth about the relationships between people and their environment.*

George is fondly remembered in Three Lakes. But his warm treatment of the community has not inspired any growth in local storytelling. Questions about local legends and lore are more likely to stop a conversation than spur a revelation.

Perhaps this silence holds no secrets. But at least one beer delivery man thinks so. He also thinks that Three Lakes' favorite booster was "in on the secret." Mike seems perplexed and insistent at the same time.

🔥 🔥 🔥

They've got a ghost down there. I've made deliveries down there for ten years. I know the beer business. I know bars. And I know when something's not right.

58

Up home in Eagle River there's always been a feeling that Three Lakes is hiding something. I don't mean everybody. Just the old guys and the store owners and the others who usually know what's going on. That writer fellow knew something about it. I overheard a cook and waitress talking about it. They acted like it was a hush-hush thing. But by that time, I already had heard the other whispers in the stock-rooms and the storage cellars.

If you listen close enough for five or six years, you start to get the drift of the whispers. Especially when you heard the word "ghost" crop up in the whispers. The writer fellow was mentioned as a source of comfort. They seemed to think he judged them blameless. But this supposed sympathy didn't seem to ease their pain, guilt, and fear of being found out.

It took a long time for a clear picture to develop. It's not like they were open about any of this. People get quiet real quick when there's any opportunity for an investigation or a lawsuit or even embarrassment in the pages of the local newspaper. When I finally put the pieces together I agreed with them. It wasn't anything sinister. It was just one of those things.

You've heard about a walk-in beer cooler where the old beer guzzlers hid after bar time? Or, as the writer put it, a place to practice ice fishing. Well, it sounds like something tragic happened in there. Something that happened, long ago. Something that led to the haunting of the cooler and of certain people in Three Lakes.

As best as I can figure, one of the old beer guzzlers was forgotten in the cooler. Then he fell asleep. When they opened the cooler up the next day the old beer guzzler was dead.

Now in the whispers around Three Lakes the talk is about "the man who froze to death." But that can't be right. He didn't freeze solid in his sleep like you would in the Arctic. More likely it was exposure. A gradual cooling of the body that shuts things down. A heart attack or stroke might have finished him off. Or he might have just stopped breathing.

Anyway that's where the ghost came from. And I guess there are a few families who feel some responsibility for this. What I can't figure out is if there is something more. Something like disposing of the body or carrying the stiff home to his own bed. There are no commonly told local stories about an odd death that would link up with this angle.

But I think it's likely. The guilt and hush-hush stuff is something you get from a coverup, not a simple accidental death. In a way you can understand it. It's sort of like a lot of hit-and-run accidents. What starts out as a screw-up leads to panic. The panic then leads to a crime. Then there's an attempt to cover up the crime. Finally others are helping with the coverup.

Anyway, the tavern ghost seems to be extremely active. It works out of area taverns. It has a good twenty-mile range. It's also popped up in resorts, supper clubs, and even convenience stores.

Of course, its preferred environment is the refrigerated unit. Not just the walk-in cooler. It's got a liking for the coolers under the bar, glass door display cases, and even frozen food cases. In the troubled families, there is the common occurrence of the head or the whole body surprising them at their homes. How would you like that when you open your refrigerator or freezer at home?

Back at the cooler where I think this all got started, there's not much said about it. Of course, they may not know about what happened. But the writer fellow must have stirred something up. There was genuine fear that he would write about it. I don't think the locals realized how much he liked the community. He may have even found some humor in the situation.

I've never seen the head or the body the way some do. But I have seen the ghost in other forms. The most common is the human shape I've seen in the cold, foggy air that drifts out of a cooler when you open a door. It's a quick-step movement that shows you he's eager to be left out. And it disappears as soon as the cold fog warms.

Then there's the face shape I've seen in condensation droplets and ice crystal patterns on cooling units. This is no Shroud of Turin or statue shedding tears. These face patterns show up at different times within different cold storage units. They even move around within units, depending on where the frost forms.

The people may be scared of this ghost. But, I don't know, he looks content in the forms I see. Just like you'd suspect of a fellow who's had a few beers.

PART III

Heart of the North

Phillips' Concrete Creepers

Ghost-hunting offers many surprises. Yet there is a tendency to assume that years of experience and dozens of encounters have prepared the investigator for every possible angle and variation. This type of comfortable arrogance is the bane of everyone who assumes they've been there, done that. But life without growth and new revelations is a simple and atrophied pond silting in before it becomes a brackish swamp.

The beginning of the journey (and many interim steps) prepared me for the possibility of connections between different northwoods spirits and inexplicable undercurrents of evil. The various offbeat, lighthearted, and warmly nostalgic ghosts along the way tended to mute the macabre and sinister spirit elements.

Word got around about my unusual quest. Unsolicited advice from self-styled seers and clairvoyants found its way onto my phone-answering machine. Letters brought sale offers concerning "special" maps and "secret" documents.

Fate finally brought me a clearer voice in the form of a friend of a friend. He was part guide, part coach, and part kick in the seat of the pants. He was on a search of his own and had thought of a few things I had missed. Robert brought me, at night, to the edge of a strange place on Highway 13 South, near Phillips.

🌿 🌿 🌿

From what everybody's telling, you're following with your nose too close to the trail. That's a good way to walk into an ambush or right up their rear ends. I saw that plenty in the Philippines back in my war. You gotta get off the trail sometimes. Off to the side.

This is not a kid's game of connect the dots or a road rally to see who can drive between ghost locations the fastest. Think it out. Take your time.

We Indians—even we unofficial ones like me—have an advantage on time. We don't hear it ticking away. We float on it like a river and get out every once in a while to look around. It was here in Phillips that I kind of climbed out of the river and looked around because something is amiss. Something is building and brewing.

You know by now that the land is as densely populated by ghosts and spirits and other unknown forces as it is by live people. Maybe more so. But if you haven't also noticed increases in strange activity and things way out of balance, then you're missing the whole point of your journey.

Think about that. What is balance? How do things get out of balance? How do we get back to balance? That view probably comes from my Ottawa background. I'm one of the last of that group in Wisconsin. The group that hung on with the Marshfield Potawatomi and then faded north into the woods.

But just because we don't have tribal picture I.D.s or enrollment certificates doesn't mean we're any less Indian. Indianness is in the heart and in the spirit. Not in who's got a share of fish or casino money. We Wisconsin Ottawa understand ghosts because we're kind of like ghosts ourselves. Hardly anybody can see us. No one's sure if we're really here. I'll bet more people believe in ghosts than believe in Ottawa.

So why did this old Ottawa bring you here? Well, not to rant and rave about the last of the Ottawa. I had to get you off your trail. Get your nose and eyes and ears off to the side. You need to look farther out on an old trail. Otherwise you loop back over your own track.

Sometimes when you're tracking you can sense the birds a mile ahead are being disturbed. The jays squawk, the crows take off from their roost. Those are chain reactions. Here we are at a part of a chain reaction. It's a thing that makes little sense on its own. But if you view it as a sign of disturbance, then it helps you judge what you're following.

What we've got here is the Wisconsin Concrete Park. Two hundred concrete figures from mythology and history. Built by old Fred Smith and left as an odd legacy to the Phillips area. It's a spooky thing to view at night. Plenty of shadows and if there's a moon, it catches the light in an eerie way.

But the real oddity here is how a place without a ghost history is pulling them in. Price County never had that much of a ghost history. Unless you go back fifty years or more to that luminous ball that kept coming out of the ground at the Fifield Cemetery. Now, Price County is drawing spirits like ants to a picnic.

This is why I want you to pay attention to what you're doing. There's serious stuff going on here. There's bigger stakes than just a couple of jokes over beers down in the flatland and a laugh at the hicks up in the pine woods. You need to decide about what you're doing. Is it a lark? Is it a tabloid search for sensationalistic meat to throw to the crowd? Or is it a real search to expand spiritual horizons?

I want you to think about what I said earlier about tracking and chain reactions. We've got ghosts by the dozens moving into concrete statues. Don't you think that tells us something? There are times at night where the concrete forms start to move. Some just rock back and forth. Some sort of dance. Others rocket straight up in the air and don't come down for hours.

Nothing bad has happened, yet. As far as I can figure, they are kind of neutral spirits. No hostile agendas or long, vengeful legacies to fulfill against the living. Just lost spirits being pulled into an old vacuum.

You not only must classify a ghost. You must determine whether it's a friend or foe or simply too damaged to help any of us. You must find the good ghosts. Find them and keep them as allies. That's right, good ghosts are the chief ally in the fight against the evil ones. Start talking to the Creator. Ask for strength. Keep yourself pure. You'll get a sign about which ones you can use or trust.

Think about what is happening here in Phillips. Ghosts are moving into inanimate objects, into material things. It's a chain reaction from things happening along your trail. But it also demands that you ask what's out of balance. Our things are coming to life. It's not right. But our things are becoming possessed.

That only happens one of two ways. It could be a curse. But that's a limited sort of one person, one object type of thing. Or there's a rip in the spirit world and they're pouring out like jellybeans out of a torn bag. That's what we've got here in Phillips. But why? And what does it mean for your journey? Will you slow down enough to figure it out?

Approach all of this with respect. Stay flexible. Keep an open mind. Quiet now. Keep still. Let's watch the statutes move.

The Trapper in the Tree

Logging ghosts are found by the hundreds throughout northern Wisconsin. Not surprising for one of the most dangerous occupations on earth. Not surprising for the enterprise that profoundly alters the landscape in a few decades and leaves a legacy of slash fires and hard-scrabble stump farming.

The human cost of felling the northwoods pinery added a grim chapter to the annals of this forestry holocaust. Nineteenth-century accounts painted a gruesome picture: mangled bodies, crushed skulls, amputations, river jockeys swept away on logjams, and crews starving and freezing to death in isolated bunkhouses.

Wisconsin has many places where you can hear logging legends and lore. The Hayward and Antigo areas have quite a few knowledgeable woodsmen who spin yarns. But perhaps the best place to capture the oldtime flavor is in Rhinelander. The Rhinelander Logging Museum acts as a magnet for those seeking to preserve the memories of the early pinery logging effort. The parklike setting with its towering trees and cabin-style building sets the mood.

There, museum volunteers and an assortment of hangers-on keep alive the folk knowledge of pre-chainsaw, pre-log skidder, and pre-truck logging. Memories of their fathers and grandfathers keep the stories fresh in their minds. Not content with the myths of Paul Bunyan, they are almost smug in the knowledge of blood relationship to real heroes.

Several visits over a ten-year period lead to a friendship with one of the museum regulars. But this acquaintance was already in its ninth year when he took me for a walk in the grove of trees where the wind in the tops hushed out the city sounds. Willard was finally ready to tell his ghost story.

🌿 🌿 🌿

The woods to the east of Rhinelander are haunted by the Trapper in the Tree. Especially out by Lake Thompson. Way out on the east end of the lake. That's where his body was found.

And what an unusual find it was too. Two men working a big cross-cut saw. They were sectioning a tree that had already been dropped.

They first hit empty space—a hollow section. Then they met odd resistance. Then they hit metal.

What it was, they broke through into a cavity. Then they cut through the mummified body. Then they sawed into his rifle. You'd better believe that they were quite surprised when they looked into that cavity. The man was preserved like a piece of dried fruit.

My grandad Jacob was one of those men. And you could easily say that he was haunted for life just on the basis of that discovery. He told the story hundreds of times. But there was more to it from him than just a sliced mummy in the tree. There had been sightings of a ghost for years before this discovery. It was said that a ghost beckoned people and motioned them to follow him. I guess he wanted his remains to be found. But who in his right mind follows a ghost? And who would think to look for a ghost in a hollow section of log twenty feet above the ground?

So how did that man come to be in that tree? Grandad knew exactly how because of the story his father told him. His father and his father's brother came in the early days. They lived on trapping until the logging jobs opened up. They ranged all the way up to the Michigan line.

In those days, not all the Indians had been pushed back into the reservations yet. There really wasn't much government up here yet to do that. Anyway, the Indians—mostly Chippewa, but some Menominee, too—still ranged through much of the forest. They trapped, too. And they really didn't like the competition.

I must be honest, too. It just wasn't the competition. The brothers here robbed some traps. So you might figure they made an enemy or two. As it turned out, the Chippewa caught up with them out near Lake Thompson. The brothers thought they'd give their pursuers the slip by splitting up. So the one brother climbed a tree to break up the trail.

On what happened next we can only speculate. The Chippewa must have gotten close and he must have discovered a hole up in the tree. So he slipped in. Then you can guess that he got stuck. The way it works in a tight vertical space is that the more you struggle, the more you sink into a tighter spot.

The other brother came back and searched. He always heard yelling on the wind in the tree tops. But he could never pin down where it was coming from. He probably thought he was already dealing with a ghost.

It's horrible to think of slow death in that tree. But it's also oddly humorous to think that body in sap could have been the biggest bug found in amber in a couple of million years if they had not cut the tree down. Gives you all sorts of opportunity to call a fellow a knothead and how he's stiff as a board.

The upshot was generations of hatred toward the Indians in my family. I'm ashamed to say that I've got grandchildren in grade school who hate Indians. Like all stories this one has two sides. Or at least another perspective. That would be the Indian perspective.

They knew something bad happened to one of the trappers. Old Indian men told me it was long thought that the trapper turned into an evil spirit and flew away. But when they learned of his fate when the tree was cut down there was an even heavier feeling. It seems that there is a feeling that a horrible death like that gives the victim the power to impose a powerful curse. With that is the sense that the cutting of the log and the body set loose some powerful bad medicine that festers and builds over time. It grows because nobody knows how to combat it.

This was certainly true in our family. The bad feelings just kept building until the explosion of hate on the boatlandings in the 1980s. That's when the tavern fights and the scuffles at basketball games started to escalate. I really think that spirit of the trapper may have moved into my son.

You could see it in his eyes: the bile, the venom, and the irrational grudges over things that are over and done. And he infected others with it. He was worked up something fierce and convinced others it was a political or justice issue. He never had an answer for me why he didn't tackle any of the thousands of other unfair situations.

From what you've told me, some groups and places have patron ghosts the way others have patron saints. You make those things sound positive, or at least harmless. But I guess here we have a different case. There can be patron evil spirits too, can't there?

The biggest question is, how does this work? Is it just some malignant natural thing loosed on us through human bumbling? Sort of like bumping a hornet's nest? Or does the evil spirit lay in wait and lure us in? Or did people with hate in their hearts stir up spirits who would otherwise rest?

Find out these things if you can. Go down to the Mole Lake Chippewa and to the Forest County Potawatomi. I'll give you a couple of names. No one wants to see me on account of my son. Let me know if we can put the Trapper in the Tree to rest and whether that will heal my son.

Crandon's Death Guide

W isconsin has many communities that appear to be torn between the poles of preservation and development. The debate is often couched in terms of a choice between the robust tackiness of the Wisconsin Dells and the forlorn abandonment of commercial and government "dead zones" of the Kickapoo Valley. This fight over development is older than we think. It goes back to at least the arrival of the French in the sixteen hundreds. Perhaps it goes back to the very beginnings of human group interaction.

In the northwoods, the land use debate has often been less about aesthetics and more about survival. There is much self-awareness among area residents about being economically marginal. There is also acknowledgment that the northwoods choice is between the hard-scrabble subsistence life and the temporary booms of extractive raw material industries. Land use conflicts, in this setting, generate passion and even hostility. They also create a cultural context and, over time, contribute to our folklore.

Crandon certainly has its quota of anger. Discussions there often boil with hard-to-understand epithets about outside tree-huggers, spearing, casinos, and the U.S. Forest Service. The thirty-year-old fight over The Mine looms over all this. In Crandon, I found it hard to find anyone who was not angry at something. In the Potawatomi lands to the east of Crandon, the anger was also evident (although more contained by a polite sullenness).

Requests for some guidance or referrals were ignored or shrugged off as if I were speaking a foreign language. I guess I was. Finally, a boy in his early teens on Sugerbush Hill told me to "go see the crazy guy up off Spring Pond Road."

The mobile home I found looked as if it had been dropped from a great height into a dense plot of aspen. An assortment of bark-covered lodges were scattered along curving paths. A dog barked from beneath a school bus body resting on stacks of railroad ties.

69

Wisk'akogabeek stepped out of the trailer, his long braids flopping as he brandished the Remington pump shotgun. The gun was lowered, but not put down, when I revealed my mission.

🌿 🌿 🌿

What'ya want? Ghosts of hate, huh? We've all got 'em. Hate goes back a long ways. Nobody knows for sure. There are angry ghosts who were angry in life. Then there are ghosts made angry by what they see the living do. Then there are natural spirits and they turn angry when they are not paid the proper respect.

I haven't figured it all out. But I think it's like what happens when you get a couple of brush fires that link up and then move up to the tops of the trees. Those combined fires are powerful fires.

We have a hateful ghost around here. I call him the Death Guide. That's because he seems to feed on anger and pull people toward destruction. An old man once told me that it was a ghost of an Iroquois enemy who tagged along with the Potawatomi. If that's true, the ghost must have followed us from Michigan near Detroit. That would've been three hundred years ago. But I guess there's no limit to how long a mad ghost stays mad.

We Potawatomi lived in mixed villages for a long time. With Huron, Ottawa, and Ojibwe. But this Death Guide was viewed as bad medicine. These other groups eventually would tell us to get lost. So we wandered further into the woods. But the Death Guide stuck with us. It even picked up more steam from other groups that didn't like us. British, Winnebago, Menominee, missionaries, and the tree rapers.

Let me tell you a story about how things work up here. It's the story about what happened after all our moving troubles and how the Death Guide settled down with us. Our culture changed through the moves and through the pressure of all the groups that didn't want us around. It was trade or starve when we first moved to Wisconsin. Then it was fight or starve when the French needed help. Then it was move to the forts or starve with the British. Then it was move or starve with the U.S. Then, finally, it was log or starve when the tree rapers came.

Each time we moved too slow for them it caused anger. When we slowed down what they called "progress" we were threatened. But a funny thing happened. The Death Guide became less of a curse to us and more of a curse on those bothering us. I guess that's how we knew this was the place to stop. You have to love this land to stay here. It's stingy and unforgiving. We need all the help we can get to hang on to what we have of our land and our culture.

Our ghost doesn't haunt an old house or cave. It doesn't wait along lonely roads ready to jump out at you. It's more of a sign. You have to understand that heaven and hell are right here. Right here among us on a parallel level. As best as I can figure, the soul's fate is determined by its balance at the moment of death. In other words, if you think you are saved, you are. If you think you are damned, you are. And if your life is in limbo, that's where you're headed.

When we see him, it means that one of the hateful people will be taken away. Whenever I see him, it's never more than three days until a funeral. So he's either an omen or a gatherer. It's usually the mean drunks. The bar fighters. The wife beaters. The guys who kick their dogs and their kids when their businesses go bankrupt. The ones who can't pay their bills and get loaded and drive into utility poles. Or the ones who are dodging child support payments and decide to blow their brains out.

They're always mad at us. Blind, raging, foaming at the mouth and mad as dogs in a pit of fleas and broken glass on the full moon. It's that same boat landing crowd that harassed the Ojibwe. The same guys who are mad at their government all the time unless it's bombing the hell out of somebody who looks different from them.

It's complicated from a ghost medicine angle. Those angry people are filled with ghosts themselves. Ghosts of cossacks that raped their grandmothers. Ghosts of the mill and foundry owners who worked their fathers to death. Ghosts of all the laughing guys in neckties and suits who send poor whites to war and call them pollocks, wops, and krauts behind their backs.

This whole thing has been a lesson to me about the poison of hate. I think it's okay to be angry 'cause anger drives change. Even Gandhi got angry. But after you get angry you gotta forgive. If you don't and your kids and grandkids don't, then you've got bad medicine that evil spirits can draw energy off of. That's what we've got here. My people have many resentments. And plenty of cause. In Crandon, the hate toward us is thick enough to cut with a chainsaw. So the Death Guide thrives and grows.

I saw the ghost the first time hovering over a boat on Wabikon Lake. It did have kind of an Indian look to it, with a scraggly Mohawk haircut. But it also had vulture wings. It turned out it was over the boat of our biggest local poacher back then. He died two days later. He just kind of hated that there were fish that somebody else might get first. He hated other fishermen. He even hated the fish.

Later, I saw the Death Guide follow the squad car of a local cop. He died pretty quick after that. Then in the 1980s, I saw the Death Guide plenty around the landings when the Mole Lake Shinnobs were spearing. We didn't have as many of the young Klu Klux Klan types like around Lac du Flambeau. We had the old guys with crew cuts with their veins bulging on their necks.

They should have been home taking their heart medicine. Instead, they were at the boat landings doing belly bumps and shouting "timber nigger" at us. I saw that old Iroquois buzzard hover over many of them. And you know, there's not many of them around anymore.

I'm working on my inner peace. And I do what I can to encourage ways for people to share this place. But as my trusty shotgun suggests, it's a fine balancing act. A warrior turned peacemaker must still be vigilant.

If we start with love and respect of the place we can build on that. If it excites you and me to watch a beaver cut a wedge through a morning's smooth, misty water and then slap his tail when the bear on the shore surprises him, then we shouldn't have to fight. That connection should unite us.

But inner peace is hard in an imperfect world. I'm not totally there yet. I have to admit that bit of gladness I feel when I see the Death Guide fly west down Highway 8 toward Crandon. There's still a smug satisfaction in me when I know he's hauling away angry redneck souls.

In my worst moments—when my spiritual power is low and when I've been called chief for the tenth time that day—I even fantasize about the Death Guide just roosting on the mining office and glaring with his hairy Iroquois eyeball at every businessman, politician, and suck-up job applicant who goes in there. I fantasize about hundreds of medicine men and women coming from all over to put a curse on those mining people and sending the Death Guide to their corporate headquarters.

So you can see. I need to work on my attitude, too.

The Herb Gatherer

Connections between the old spiritual traditions and contemporary incidents involving unusual phenomena are common in northwoods Indian country. The real trick is sorting out the interpretations of these traditions and getting to a core of eyewitness observations.

The journey had thus far exposed me to a variety of American Indian teachings. Ojibwe influence was particularly strong, and I also found Ottawa and Potawatomi lore still surviving. The stories I heard were not always consistent with the anthropological accounts or with the "official" Midewin teachings. Yet, my sources were sincere. Did this mean that certain information was intentionally suppressed or inadvertently ignored by "authorities?"

A Mole Lake source thinks so. He suspects that European-Americans and Indians share the blame for lost and buried knowledge. He is not a natural candidate for information on ghosts or other paranormal phenomena. His knowledge of physical and biological sciences sets him apart from many others at Mole Lake. He often quotes scientific journals and identifies plants by their Latin and Ojibwe names.

Jerry is guarded in his remarks out of his concern for his job at an intertribal agency. Our conversation occurs in a Crandon coffee shop under suspicious stares of other patrons and the hostile glaring eyes of counter staff who serve him only because of my presence.

So the "ghost man" comes to talk to me. At Mole Lake it is like you've heard elsewhere. There are many ghosts. Most harmless. But some think that the bad ones are acting up.

I've heard the elders implicate ghosts in everything from drug trafficking and arrests to diarrhea at the casino. And we've had some tribal officials who are supposed to be haunted, too. Talk always comes back to the role of "the Mine." There are ghosts at the County B gravel pit. Some at the Crandon airport. Others at Swamp Creek and Bishop Lake.

I can talk later about these if you want and give you contacts for others. But I think the one I know best is the one that has the most bearing on your work. I call him "the herb gatherer." My Grandmother Suzette called him "bagaanaak"—the hazelnut. I think that was because the hazelnut was prized for its threefold service as food, medicine, and drumstick wood.

Now to get to what I have to tell you, I have to tell you a story. I'll bet you're getting tired of Indians saying that, aren't you? Did you know that Winona—the mother of all—had a son named Nanabojo? She died shortly after birth and the child was raised by his grandmother Nokomis.

Nokomis, for the first time, taught secret women's knowledge to a man. Nanabojo was the first man to learn of the medicine within plants. Before that, medicine was thought of only as an aid to prayers. As in burning or smoking the cedar, sage, or tobacco. Now a man understood that the plants could heal the body and invigorate the mind. Nanabojo, in turn, taught many women about the medicine plants. But kept it as a special gift to them from the Great Spirit. That's how it went for a long time.

Then one day, right at Mole Lake, a medicine man wanted to learn these women's secrets. So he followed them to where Nanabojo was teaching. And he dressed as a woman in order to fool Nanabojo. But Nanabojo was wise to the trick. He gave the medicine man a special plant that sent him over to the spirit world. This is how the herb gatherer or bagaanaak became a ghost that is allowed to come back only to help men understand plant medicine.

The herb gatherer was explained to me by my grandmother. But she had never seen him. Only a few of the old Mide priests had ever seen him. But I first saw him in a dream. Then I saw him the first time I smoked the pipe. And I saw him again when I did my first sweat lodge.

My grandmother said these were all signs that I was to study this plant knowledge. So I did, including university level botany. When I returned from my training and internships, I saw the herb gatherer at the end of Black Joe Road. That's where he first talked to me and confirmed everything my grandmother had said.

Over the last four or five years, I have had dozens of conversations with him. And I think I've learned quite a bit about him and his place in the greater scheme of things. He introduced me to the notion of ghost as time traveler. He said the plant given to him by Nanabojo is the key to time travel.

Unfortunately, evil ghosts have just about wiped that plant out in their lust to control humans and make their lives miserable. He told me that these malignant spirits whisk back and forth as French traders, English soldiers, politicians, and businessmen on the power of this plant. Somewhere, in some time period, they've got a big hoard of the plant.

In order to use this stuff, you have to be willing to give up your physical being. If you use it enough and in the proper way, it will first allow out-of-body experiences and then eventually your spirit will be able to move about at will. The herb gatherer says it may even allow space travel.

You'd think that the fact that evil spirits have gotten this power would have spiritual people up in arms. But it's kind of quiet. But there are other factors at work. Some think this thing sounds like a mind-altering drug. Some think we'll get blamed for it, like tobacco. And there's always the fear of driving business away from resorts and casinos. Plus the medicine men don't want to admit that they don't know how to control this stuff. They don't understand how it works.

Then the tribal officials don't want to think about the political implications of this plant. They're trying to hide the fact that this resource would be covered by the treaties. It is, after all, a plant gathered traditionally that was present in ceded territory. Think of it. DNR has to protect it. Wardens have to drive off the illegal harvests. A system of quotas and distribution must be devised. What an uproar all that would cause.

They all know that this fight is tougher than fighting for fish. And it goes even deeper than fighting to protect water and air. It is the ultimate ecological issue—the struggle against evil as it poisons everything. We need to fight it the same way you always fight evil. You apply even more good in opposition to it.

Good people need to recover and restore the plant. Then they must master it. They must use it to cross over in great numbers to neutralize the evil. The herb gatherer is helping me learn how to go about it. It's his way of making up for turning this thing loose.

He brought me this vision of the place where the plant still grows. There is a fern-carpeted glen with a cool bubbling spring. It is at the head of a hemlock-lined valley. There the plant grows. When I find it, I'll let you know. It might help you find the answers you're looking for. I'll ask the herb gatherer if I can share it with you.

Hidden Graves on Timm's Hill

W*isconsin's geological mounds are focal points for much lore—ghost and otherwise. These high points offer legends which have roots in the era immediately after the glacial retreat. Sites such as Blue Mounds, Sinsinawa, and Wildcat Mountain evoke strong feelings about the sacredness of place. They figure as ceremonial locations for ancient American Indians and pioneer European Christians.*

Most of these "mounds" are in southwest Wisconsin. There, they are generally seen in a positive light despite hauntings and covert ceremonies. Some are thought to have inspired the area's effigy mounds.

Timm's Hill is definitely outside the belt of promontories found in the driftless region. It also offers the flip side of "mound" lore: the mass grave. Dozens of hillocks and ridges in the lake and marsh country are rumored to be home to the remains of victims of massacres, battles, serial killers, and ghoulish cannibals. Some, like Butte des Morts, have a firm footing in well-known accounts. Other tales are obscure and elusive.

Timm's Hill certainly rises above obscurity. At 1,951 feet, it is Wisconsin's highest point. It is visited by many seeking its tower view of Price, Taylor, Lincoln, and Rusk counties. But at least one local resident feels there is more than stately basswoods and graceful birches. Mike, an artisan from the Town of Spirit, to the east of Timm's Hill, shares a story uncovered from musty attic trunks.

🔥 🔥 🔥

My family has a five-generation relationship with Timm's Hill. So you could call us pioneer stock. Dad's family came up here early. Mom's people were French out of Green Bay and Oconto. Probably part Menominee, although they make an insistent claim that they're pure French that flys in the face of their high cheekbones and shiny black hair.

The family always had ghost stories about Timm's Hill. Headless loggers. Lost oxen drivers. Sort like that. But they told them in the same warm and familiar way as the other local ghost tales. Like the Mundeaux Creek ghost, the Spirit Lake swimmers, or the Mackeys Spur signalman.

Grandad hinted at darker things. He'd mention the bodies at Timm's Hill. But grandma would hush him and tell him not to scare the kids. It wasn't until a few years ago—when I inherited the old house on Highway 102—that I learned anything more about those childhood stories. The answers were up in the attic.

That attic was not a place I was looking forward to. It was a family joke that it was last cleaned when Roosevelt was President. And they always left it an open question as to which Roosevelt. But it was definitely not the kind of place that a middle-aged guy with asthma would go to recuperate.

Grandad had a sailor's trunk up there. He sowed his wild oats on the lake steamers. He was with Dewey at Manila and helped land the Marines that threw the old queen out of Hawaii. So I expected to find seaman's items and exotic souvenirs. Instead, there were some heavy old Navy revolvers. Newspaper clippings from Chicago about gangster killings. And bundles of photos and letters.

It turned out Grandad knew those criminals who hid out at Manitowish Waters and Little Bohemia. Dillinger and that crowd. And, as much as I hate to implicate a grandparent in anything criminal, I guess I have to say Grandad was probably helping them dispose of bodies on Timm's Hill. What can you say about such a thing? Would you talk about how some of those criminals were considered Robin Hoods? Or was it just a way for Grandad to pick up money during tough times?

But that was not the end of the family saga about Timm's Hill. Way back under the other attic junk was an old wooden chest that took the story back to pioneer days. It was my great-great-grandfather's chest. Sturdy hardwood box with heavy leather straps. Quite a valuable antique, actually.

Inside were some of the tools you'd expect. Hoof-trimming and horseshoe items. But also other things. Like some touching letters from this nearly forty-year-old, bewildered man telling his wife of the terrible carnage of men and horses on some battlefield in the South. And like some business accounts that suggest that my family did have many dealings with those French-Menominee mixed bloods even before grandma happened along.

But for your purposes, the most interesting thing in that chest was an old map with many notations. Aside from the notes, there were series of geometric shapes between points—mostly triangles—on the map and a number of heavily inked lines from Timm's Hill to other places. One line ran to Strawberry Island at Lac du Flambeau. Another to Lac Vieux Desert. And real heavy multiple lines from Timm's Hill to Crandon and Portage. There were also arrow lines up on Rib Mountain at Wausau and Bell Mound over by Black River Falls.

The map looked as if it had seen a lot of use. A lot of folding and camp fire sparks. The notes were hard to figure. Timm's Hill was labeled a negative pole. A little chart listed times of heavy northern lights activity and how much those incidents altered compass readings at Timm's Hill.

I wish you could study the map closer. But we had a break-in and it was taken. Random theft or a competitor for you, who knows? But take those other things with you. See if you can make some sense of them. There's stuff about the Menominee cannibals and cannibals eating victims out at Timm's Hill. Maybe when you get down to Keshena they can tell you about that.

Somehow it's related to the windigo or wendeeko—the flesh-eating giants of the old Algonquin stories. But here it's ghosts or spirits—hate-filled ones—that move into live humans and turn them into cannibal zombies. And this is all done on some schedule related to the northern lights.

Have I seen any zombie cannibals? Well, no. But let me tell you about being up on that tower at night during a northern lights display. Even by starlight I could see strong winds whipping the trees at lower levels. Yet there was an eerie calm up on the tower. Each time the northern lights pulsed there was a pulsing on the hill. Like a squirming mass of worms.

The tower took on a green glow. Luminous globes came up out of the ground—they sure looked like heads. So, strange force? You bet!

Ladysmith's Conjured-up Ghosts

The impressions created by my visit to the Crandon area weighed on my mind as I made a leisurely drive on U.S. Highway 8 toward Ladysmith. Maybe mining poisoned a place even before the first shovel of dirt was turned. Maybe the poison of Indian-hating, and treaties, and who gets the walleyes seeps into the ground and makes mining even more hazardous.

Many of the Crandon conditions were present in Ladysmith. The main difference was that the mining had already started to make its enormous incision on the bank of the Flambeau River. A stubborn core of anti-mine prophets kept vigil in Ladysmith. They had lost their fight to stop the mine. They were struggling to avoid the weariness of the perpetual ELF protests.

My Crandon sources suggested that the Ladysmith group was approaching the spiritual dimension of their protest in a pro-active manner. There was a rumor of a plan to invoke spirits and activate them against the mine. My instructions sent me to Riverside cemetery to await an informant. The daylight waned and the lengthening graveyard shadows merged into a dark blanket.

A small beat-up foreign car inched up behind me and its parking lights flicked off. A woman in a long Guatemalan peasant dress left the car and joined me in my truck. We sat in the dark truck cab. Sarah talked of lessons learned and warned about careless stirring of the spirit pot.

🌿 🌿 🌿

The political people think we failed. But I learned a great deal. Foremost, that we were going about our task in the wrong way and with the wrong attitude.

As you probably heard, it was our intent to invoke local spirits, ghosts, and manitous and direct them against those connected with the mine. You might call it a curse or a hex. On that level, it was a symbolic act. Like back in the Sixties when the Yippies surrounded the Pentagon in an effort to levitate it.

In another way, you might look at it as psychological warfare. I think some of us thought there might be some voodoo effect on some of the mine staff. You know, heightened anxiety and psychosomatic symptoms. But I really think that among those of us directly working the "spirit angle"—as it came to be called by the political activists— there was a serious commitment to cause a psychic and spiritual disturbance. That's where we went wrong.

We had the assembled power, the right people resources. We had many people with abilities as mediums and spirit conduits. We had a Hmong shaman, celtic pagans, Wiccan priestesses, eco-feminist rabbis, an expelled Amish herb doctor, some defrocked clergy, and many tribal medicine men. I must say it was a powerful combination.

There was a cumulative effect that none of us had ever felt before. A synergy or resonance that was unbelievable.

And it worked. My, my, did it work. We invoked spirits by the dozens. Almost every significant soul dwelling in or about the Flambeau River came bubbling up in our ceremonies, our campfires, and our dreams. But there was one big surprise. There was a very powerful grandmother spirit that was dredged up along with all the ghosts and lesser manitous. Some of the Chippewa elders said it was Nokomis herself—the Grandmother of Everything.

The significance of this situation was that this grandmother spirit controlled all of the subservient ghosts and manitous. This control had serious implications. She—the grandmother spirit—just would not allow us to do what we set out to do. And she would not allow the other spirits to act for us either.

She forced us to go into direct communication with her. Did she ever lay down the law to us! It was like being caught spilling juice on your grandma's parlor carpet. This started a learning process for us. We learned many things about how specific ghosts operate and what capabilities individual spirits possess.

In a way, we came to see the grandmother spirit as the conductor of a great orchestra. We may have previously known how to conjure up a ghost. But now we could see that such a simple act was as modest as one note played on a single instrument. The ghosts here at the cemetery are mobile and have detective type skills. The river ghosts are mostly guardians. The woods ghosts have special relationships with the animals.

She let us know that we were flirting with evil ourselves. She saved us from ourselves. We came close to crossing the line between white magic and black magic. Our hearts were poisoned. She let us know that it all starts in the heart. That's right. Those of us who would commune with spirits and work "magic" here in the material world need to purify our hearts with love.

She taught us that in a conflict like we have here, you start toward that love by first acknowledging you have an enemy. You confront the humiliation of your own hatred. You admit to God, the Great Spirit, the Great Pumpkin, or whatever, that this hatred is in you. Then you pray, meditate, or chant, or whatever. You embrace that enemy in prayer and call blessings down on them.

So when you get to the space where you are invoking spirits and conjuring up souls to do work, your heart is in the right place. She taught us to use God's generosity and His greater vision. She taught us to first use summoned spirits to transform our most closely held hatreds. In doing this, many of us found new and deep reservoirs of love. We became instruments of grace and healing. We called for blessings on those who brought the mine here.

Now in our ceremonies, we call for the joining of the mine people to the community of those caring for the earth. We pray that they be dealt with compassionately and that they be granted wisdom and prudence. We pray that their hatred of us be tempered so that it does no harm to them or the earth. The spirits we invoke are now sent on missions to safeguard the mine. They now serve as guardians and instruments of this concern.

You might ask whether this changes anything. Well, they haven't voluntarily shut the mine. They haven't brought herbal tea and organic cookies over to the protesters. But I sense some vigilance. I hope it's there. I hope we are convincing them of the absolutely essential role they have, impressing on them just how much depends on them, and instilling in them awe and reverence for the protective functions. That's what I pray.

Will it work? It's too early to tell. Maybe in fifty years it will be too early to tell. But it's the right track. The ghosts we now conjure up protect our corner of the earth. You know from your visits elsewhere that the opposite is happening in many places.

Learn from our mistakes. What we did almost backfired. Not all of the evil that is abroad comes from evil intent. Even bumbling can put things out of balance. We're all in danger. From ghosts and the living. Our prayers and our ghosts go with you.

Feast of the Dead

European-American folklore contains many prescriptions for communication with the spirit world and seasonal timetables for such encounters. These old beliefs and practices echo in the form of Halloween celebrations and seances.

American Indian practices seem more individualized and private. The relationship with spirits is usually direct and unmediated.

A medicine man might offer counsel or assistance. But in the end, the vision or the dream is an intensely personal experience. Such observations on my part created the impression that American Indian customs lacked group interaction within celebrations of ghosts.

My further education came close on the heels of the Ladysmith encounter. Each day now brought hints of individuals and whole subcultures working on questions of interest to my quest. There was a hidden network of spiritually attuned northwoods activists under the layers of homesteaders, ecologists, and tribal traditionalists.

I began to see signs that poking around for ghosts was no longer a harmless hobby. Questions led to backlash. My truck was run off the road near Glen Flora and near Spirit Falls. A night in a friend's cabin on Old Veteran Lake in Marinette County was punctuated by a rifle shot through the door.

My contact with this emerging northwoods network of the spiritually-attuned heightened my caution. They asked me to be discreet in my public inquiries. They made me aware of a spiritual underground railroad and advised me to "ride" it. They even steered me to "station." A "conductor" took me to Wabeno. From there, I was blindfolded and put in the back of a van. A short ride took us off pavement. There was a heavy perfume of balsam fir and a whiff of brackish water.

The van stopped. I was gently unloaded. A kind hand nudged my head down through a low passage. A fire crackled and bodies shifted. I knew that I was in a bark lodge. The blindfold was lifted. Floyd looked into my blinking eyes to assess my well-being.

🌿 🌿 🌿

Hope you're okay. You must have many questions. Like who are we? We're a new tribe. Don't laugh! We have lots of Chippewa and Potawatomi blood here. And the ever-present Cherokee octoroons and whites with Indian hearts. This is a tribe set up to help people survive the cleansing time. The time when the earth is made over. So we have an interest in making sure the spirits are in balance for us.

You come at a special time. It is our Feast of the Dead, the time when you can form direct relationships with spirits. Relationships that build your strength and stay with you all your life. At one time, the Feast of the Dead was only conducted at the time of building the summer villages, the time of the "Strawberry Moon." But now we know how to do them for each season.

The Feast of the Dead came to the Ojibwe from the Ottawa. But the Ottawa were taught it by the Huron. There lies the tale. Hurons were at one time part of the Iroquois. But they learned to do things with the Feast of the Dead that the Iroquois did not approve of. This is where the bad blood came from. This is where hundreds of years of war came from.

We honor our ghosts. We make food for them. We sing and dance for them. We even play games for them. And they come back to teach us. They tell us the stories that have been forgotten.

The stories are everything. All the answers are there. All the wisdom to keep us safe in the future is there. I once heard a Shinnob from Red Cliff say that we should offer to take the radioactive waste site because ten thousand years from now, we would be the only ones who would tell the stories about where and what it is and what the danger signs meant.

I won't be able to tell you the story of the Feast of the Dead in one night. But you will get to see how this works. Forget everything you've ever heard about where ghosts live. You need to understand the geography of the spirit world.

I've heard that sociologists talk about how our outlook places us in both vertical and horizontal planes of spiritual space. That means that everything connects and that if you work on it, you can touch those other planes. I'm going to give you an exercise for touching those planes. First, we'll cleanse you with burning sage. Now close your eyes. You'll feel light touches. Relax.

You're no longer the bystander. No longer the curious guy playing a scavenger hunt for ghosts. No, this is for real. You're part of the dynamic now. Part of what's stirring things up. That old sociology problem. When you study something close up you become part of it and change it. But don't even think of stopping. You're in this until the end like the rest of us. It's too late to go home to your farm and act as if your journey never happened.

They are in the lodge with us now. They are on both sides of you. Old ones. They're here to touch your mind. You'll feel them. You're in their hands now. Feel the hands on your chest. You shake as if you've never been touched by a spirit before. Relax.

You've brought out the old trapper, the French trader, and the warriors. They're here for you. They are here to give you a vision of your totem. They will give you a gift of an animal spirit. A strong one to guide you. One to protect you.

Right now the lodge is filling up like never before. The old medicine men ghosts. The great hunters. It is a good night and they welcome the feast. Honor their presence in your prayers. Ask that the Creator make you worthy of all those who come here tonight. Ask the Creator to grant you the strength and insight to finish your journey.

Your totem is taking shape. You are taking its shape. You start to see its bright eyes. Feel the sharp fangs within your lips. Feel the claws in your palms. Keep this creature in your heart. Tell no one what it is. Call it when you need it.

Now open your eyes and meet the spirits that have filled this lodge to help us learn the stories needed to get us through the cleansing time.

Porte Des Morts' Angry Dead

Door County's reputation is sufficiently idyllic and pastoral that one hardly thinks of ghosts at all, much less malevolent ghosts. Yet, even this scenic peninsula has dark undercurrents flowing from disputes over use of the land.

The peninsula is loaded with maritime ghosts: a drowned fisherman at Shoemaker Point, several swept-away children at Clay Banks, boatyard ghosts at Sturgeon Bay, false lights at Sherwood Point, Potawatomi canoe spirits at Eagle Bluff, and shipwrecked goblins at Ellison Bay. Ethnic flavor is also present: Belgian cobbler ghosts in Brussels, a phantom New England peddler in Ephraim, a French voyageur in Sister Bay, and a Norwegian pioneer in Gills Rock.

A lead on a more ominous spirit brought me to Northport. But the local eccentrics offered no more than cryptic commentary. It looked like I was at a dead end. Only hot tea in the restaurant overlooking the channel offered any solace.

Events then took a strange turn. A theft of a bag from my truck prompted a pursuit. A ride on the ferry during rough weather. A near fall off the ferry. A bump on the head on the steel deck. But it was a sequence that brought me straight to Joshua at the Detroit Harbor landing. It was odd to see a distinguished looking white-haired man

*standing in the rain with my bag. But it was odder still that he had a
story for me.*

🔥 🔥 🔥

By your look, I am guessing I have something that belongs to you.
Come. Let's get you dried off. I intercepted our little island thief. My
granddaughter has a problem. She often grabs things out of unlocked
cars on the mainland.

I peeked in your bag and saw your notes. Some strange things, I
must say. I have an interest in peculiar things myself. Of course, I'm
too old to chase around like you're doing. That's a young man's game.
You try to work smarter instead of harder when you get to be my age.
You learn to be a bit more cautious. At least I learned that when the
church encouraged me to take early retirement.

I could regale you for hours with odd stories from the area. Some-
time you should investigate the glowing stones of Rock Island. And
the howling on Detroit Island. Or the creeping vapors on Little Lake.
Your European-American perspective on ghosts won't be complete
until you understand our Icelandic spirits. Fishermen and sailors, old
country spirits, and haunted Viking longboats.

But those things can wait. You need to focus on the main event.
You need to understand the channel and the bluff. There are more
ghosts in Porte des Morts than anywhere else in North America. Maybe
in the world. In order to understand why there are so many, you need
to understand the role of Washington Island. It is a special refuge.

This role began after the last ice age. There were once cave paint-
ings that showed this history, but the cave collapsed. Whenever there
was a surge of evil in the Great Lakes area, the opponents of evil sought
sanctuary on the island. Each time, evil-doers followed them up the
peninsula. Each time the channel claimed the lives of the evil-doers
when they attempted to cross over to the island.

The first time involved the predecessor tribe of the Winnebago.
Back in those days, they were called the Red Banks people. Hostile
southern tribes pursued them up to the island and prepared to lay siege
with thousands of warriors. Porte des Morts swallowed them in a
whirlpool. Later, the Menominee took refuge there from the Sioux.
When the Sioux attempted to cross, an early ice storm came up and
froze hundreds of them in their canoes.

85

Then with the Iroquois invasion, the Potawatomi sought refuge on Washington Island. This was in the middle sixteen hundreds. The Iroquois sent thousands onto the waters of Porte des Morts. A violent storm, complete with waterspouts, sent each and every Iroquois warrior to the bottom.

All this served to intensify the power of the channel. The thousands of angry dead made the place more volatile. Yet, surprisingly, the place is not threatening to your average person.

There is quite a bit I don't understand about how this all works. Why do the evil dead expend their wrath on live evil people instead of those fighting evil? Why does it require a critical mass to trigger the channel's power?

It has something to do with how evil amplifies and magnifies itself. Maybe something of a boomerang effect, too. A matter of evil begetting evil? There's an individual response triggered by malignant people. Some see rotted corpses rising out of the depths. Some see skeletons draped in lake weeds. Others see the death masks of the old Iroquois.

Small groups of hatemongers trigger some slight responses. A group of skinheads had their boat capsized. And an outing of corporate attorneys who specialize in fighting environmental regulation gashed their sailboat on the rocks. But no really big Old Testament stuff like what happened with the Iroquois. It has made me wonder if Porte des Morts can be sprung like a trap. I believe that if sufficient number of haters, destroyers, and sociopaths are lured into the channel, we can trigger this large booby trap.

The question is, how do we get the militia and freemen types to come as a group? How do we get those mean-spirited types who use religion as a club, and all the immigrant-baiters to hold their conventions here? How do we get the assorted Indian-haters, fast-buck developers, toxic dumpers, wise-use charlatans, and sagebrush rebellion crackpots to plan to come out here for a big anti-government rally?

It probably says something about why my career as a pastor came to an end that I have these thoughts. But I suppose I reached my tolerance level for hypocrisy and venality. So if there's ever a way to arrange for a large excursion boat of Rush Limbaugh fans to come this way on some gray fall day, let me know what I can do to facilitate their trip.

The Wolf River Sportsman

Wisconsin's ghostly outdoorsmen usually originate at least two or three generations back. Where they are not clearly from the pioneer era, they range from simple rustics to profane rednecks. At first blush there is no obvious connection of such traditional tales to the deeper spiritual currents and problems of supernatural imbalance. How do these "typical" Wisconsin ghosts fit with the dark side?

The earlier parts of my northwoods journey focused so much on the history, folklore, and ethnic components of the ghost stories that I had missed much about the ghosts of recent origin. The tales like those about the Ice Fisherman and Three Lakes Cooler Ghost touched upon contemporary ghosts that fit within traditonal spirit categories. They left me wondering if there were any stories that linked these traditions to the disturbance patterns found among my more agitated sources.

An unusual source offered me "fresh sightings" of a brand spanking new ghost and a new perspective on a spot which had long magnified spirit energy. He was a recently retired political "insider." The type of person no one heard much about. His fingerprints were on every significant state government deal of the prior forty years.

We sat on the screened-in porch of his cedar log cabin near Pickerel's Big Twin Lake. The ice in the drinks melted and the stars were reincarnated in a purple sky as I waited for Raymond to speak.

I first saw this ghost last summer in the state fishery area south of Pickerel. I knew who it was right away. He looked alive. I spoke to him. But he did not answer. He just kept casting.

For your purposes, we will call him the "Wolf River Sportsman." He would like that. He fancied himself a sportsman even though he spent far more time in boardrooms than in the field or on the streams. He was someone I knew for fifty years. Back to our days on campus at Madison. We were both young hard-chargers when the Progressive Party broke up. We were in on all the subsequent plots and cabals.

Through the years, we were sometimes collaborators and sometimes adversaries. Sometimes we could not tell if we were on the same side or not. Sometimes our roles switched in the middle of a transaction. But through it all, we remained good friends. We often met for drinks at his Madison Club or my Wisconsin Club in Milwaukee. We managed to squeeze in a fishing trip together every few years.

Naturally, I was surprised to see him as a ghost up here. At first, I expected the *Christmas Carol* type of clanking chains and warning of past indiscretions. But I guess he thought I am honest enough to figure those things out. So while he talks to others, he just grunts at me.

Other people started to see him too. Some who recognized him. At first, all here on the Pickerel stretch of the Wolf. Later, I saw him all the way down to Markton in southeast Langlade County. Some of his other friends have even seen him down in Marquette and Adams counties.

That made him seem like that Pecatonica fisherman in southwest Wisconsin that you wrote about. The gentleman ghost sort of thing. But with differences. Here, the long-time residents say he is displacing the older ghosts. They say he has run off the ghosts that were present at every rapids on the Wolf. Temporarily or permanently? Stronger ghostly energy or just plain dominant personality?

What is he doing up here? Well, that is a complicated question. At one time, he owned thousands of acres up here. Land that accrued—or maybe I should say "accreted"—to him through years of deals. But partly it is the Crandon Mine. He was in the backrooms of that deal in ways that few would imagine. At least for someone so intimately connected to the modern conservation movement.

His life was a study in gray. Movers and shakers know the illusion of black or white. I would wager that most ghosts are black or white in terms of good or evil. Not this one. Pure gray.

A harsh judge might hand all the major environmental compromises in this state around his neck. Some might say that he did more—albeit unintentionally—to cause the rift between the people and the Department of Natural Resources than anyone in this state. What can I say? He had connections. He was paid well to use them. He did much good.

Did he help himself and his friends out along the way? Sure. If you are well-enough connected you can make sure that the state buys your favorite fishing areas and preserves them for all time. Maybe you make a little money for your inconvenience in arranging this.

Wisconsinites do not like to admit this happens. But if they want a squeaky-clean government above all else, they should have kept the

Progressives, instead of falling for the drunken hysteria of Joe McCarthy. You get what you deserve.

So I think the sportsman is here partly because of his feelings about all the deals. The mine. Paper company windfalls. Water quality compromises. All the things that threaten his beloved Wolf River.

There are other considerations too. He had ties to powerful law enforcement interests. The connect-the-dots game that is played out between police, judges, and prosecutors. Some coverups, some setups. He was queasy over the apparent accidents and suicides.

But if you are looking for things out of balance because of evil, you will not find them here. Sometimes imbalance comes from confusion, ambivalence, and inattention. It was those three things that caused the collapse of Progressive politics in Wisconsin.

So for our sportsman here, it could be the usual ghost track of unresolved business. Or torment over what might have been. But I think I now understand that you can be consigned to ghost status because of the expectations of others. Just as in life, the general perception guides reality.

Maybe you end up damned and haunting a place because of the power of your image or even the subconscious ill-will directed your way. Maybe the haunting is in us, the living. Maybe we activate it. So maybe I activated my sportsman. I had a hand in all the same deals.

The Special's Ghost

The observations of the "insider" at Pickerel raised the interesting possibilities about influence peddling in the afterlife. Did it mean that ghosts could be "corrupt" as well as "spooky?" Did it mean that power possessed on the physical plane could be transferred to the spirit world?

Again, I discovered that I was not the only one thinking about such problems. A call from my Timm's Hill source sent me scurrying to Pelican Lake. It was my first substantial backtracking on what had been, so far, a southern course. My Timm's Hill contact told me I was to meet a new source at a logging road in the Pratt Junction Marsh south of Pelican Lake. There I would supposedly hear a fantastic story about a conservation warden's ghost who was still battling wrongdoing.

My new informant was late for his end of the workday appointment. A beautiful sunset later compensated for the delay. An osprey family in circular flight in the red twilight almost made me forget why I was there. After dark, my concern was reactivated. Did I have the wrong day?

The Pelican Lake source never showed up. Several other tips did corroborate the ghost warden account. Yet the location kept shifting. A report from Burma Road in central Lincoln County maintained that the ghost warden had caused the crash of a carload of deer poachers. A report from near Gleason claimed that a car-ramming incident on Hall Road left an illegal fish spearer with whiplash and hysteria.

The confusion forced me to seek advice from someone outside the northwoods proper. A few inquiries convinced me that I needed to talk to someone who not only knew the whole territory, but also knew the ins and outs of conservation law enforcement. A referral took me backtracking southward to Poynette. There Joe, a retired conservation warden with thirty-five years of experience up north, greeted me from a farmhouse porch overlooking Mud Lake.

🌿 🌿 🌿

I hate to break the news to you. You're not tracking a conservation warden, you're tracking a "special." A special is an assistant to a warden. Sort of a part-time, seasonal deputy.

Now as a retired warden, I usually don't put wardens second to anybody. Call us popple cops or trout police if you want. But we are the thin green line in the bush. Part crusading knights, part avenging angel of Mother Earth, and part frontier marshal. We end up in the center of every rural conflict.

But a big part of who we were and what we are is tied to the specials. Almost all the old hard-nosed wardens started as specials. I did. Wardens were fond of their specials and tried to pick the brawniest, yet level-headed and personable fellows they could find. This special's ghost is from one of the best. He for sure would have been a warden, probably a darn good one. Maybe chief warden.

He died during undercover work up north. Work that was never officially recognized by the department. He had infiltrated a big poacher group that was selling deer, illegal beaver, fish, and waterfowl. The group had ties to organized crime. There were crooked sheriffs involved in this and politics too. His family never got a death benefit.

The ring was running various parts of their operations around Eagle River, Three Lakes, Pelican Lake, Gleason, and a big belt between Merrill and Rib Lake. And it just so happens that those are the areas where the special's ghost is seen. This is where he uses the old-time warden method of car-ramming to knock violators out of commission. You should see the looks on the faces of those hoodlums when they say that their trucks were battered and pushed off the road by old Packards or Hudsons.

The special's ghost still has a nose for undercover work too. You might say he's one of the reasons why wardens have a cautious attitude toward other law enforcement agencies, especially up at the federal level. Along with bizarre incidents like over in the Sauk City area, where a police officer executed a suspect right in front of a warden's eyes.

We like to assist in legitimate law enforcement, but we don't understand what's happening in some places. Some police agencies are loaded down with crazy guys who claim to have been secret agents for military intelligence. Others belong to wacky militia groups. I've met some who told me that the CIA implanted secret devices in their bodies. Which in the beginning, I took as evidence of their craziness.

But the special's ghost taught me different. He still arranges for evidence of crimes to show up on the doorsteps of us old wardens. Good special that he is, he leaves it up to us to figure out which law enforcement contacts can be trusted.

But he threw some stuff my way that raised the hair on the back of my neck. It's come in several file folders, some manila envelopes, and one big banker's record box. Stuff about a fifty-year secret project in northern Wisconsin. Stuff about harnessing the earth's magnetic field. The government started it in World War Two. They made a whole ship invisible and had it reappear hundreds of miles away. It was supposed to be a secret weapon. Then they moved their work to the Bermuda Triangle.

When they got to the next phase, they moved to northern Wisconsin. That's when they expanded from regular science into paranormal research. The change came because they discovered that living tissue could not withstand this use of electromagnetic energy. A spirit is, in essence, a charge. It can move in these electrical fields.

Yeah, that's their obsession with the ghosts. They're trying to use them as soldiers in this energy field. Only problem is that it's run out of control for them. That's why we've got people in the boondocks with human skin lampshades and body parts in their refrigerators.

You see, they moved to northern Wisconsin because it was isolated and yet didn't have missile silos and other vulnerable weapons systems. But they forgot the basics. They forgot about the electric power transmission grid. And they didn't anticipate the development of cable TV, microwave relays, and cellular phones. Then there's the usual government routine of the left hand not knowing what the right hand is doing. So another branch of the government gave them ELF.

This is when things started to bust loose. All their killer spirits could move around through the earth's crust and up through ground wires. From there, they can move up electric wires, through phones and computers. Coming in as our kids watch TV. Hell, they can even bounce off communication satellites. It's like an out-of-control computer virus now.

So we've got all these G. Gordon Liddy types who volunteered to be killed so that they could fight the evil empire as ghosts in the electromagnetic field. But hell, now they themselves are the evil empire. You can't tell the players without a scorecard. We have the live CIA trying to stop the zombie CIA they've created. We have the big corporations trying to figure out how to exploit the time travel and space travel potential of these discoveries. And we have foreign intelligence agents trying to figure out how much of the U.S. government has been subverted by the electronic zombies.

The big problem is sorting through the distractions and boobytraps. The government doesn't want panic, so it creates other rumors. You know, the cattle mutilations, black United Nations helicopters, and alien abductions. Then they have their plants in the various police and sheriff's departments in order to keep tabs on locals who might figure it out.

The special's ghost has brought us the information on all of this. I believe the special's ghost is the only force working against these things. It would be a good thing if we could figure out how he works and organize our own little resistance army with him. Can we sign you up?

Hay River Hellraiser

Farmer ghost story fragments are more common in southern Wisconsin than in the northwoods. Stories from both areas are dripping with the sadness that flows from farm foreclosures, maiming accidents, unrewarded hard work, and quiet poverty. Northwoods farmer ghosts have additional traditions connected to logging and mining. Their spirits inhabit space within the legacies of fights with powerful economic interests and the struggles to eke out a living on ruined land.

Perhaps it was inevitable that such conditions would produce a ghost of an activist bent. The surprise was in the recent origin of the spirit. The tale of the Wolf River sportsman should have prepared me for ghosts arising from among our contemporaries. But somehow I continued to follow the view of spirits as comfortably distant in time and place.

The idea of a modern activist ghost flowing from a recent activist life did not occur to me. The notion that it would arise from someone I knew and worked with would have seemed farfetched. Yet, it now seems so natural. Here, no touchy-feely guides popped up to help me. No stoic American Indian spiritual advisers prepared my path. My trip to the Hay River country was inspired by an unfriendly source. An adversary of nearly twenty years duration called to demand a meeting. Only his assurance of solid connection to my current endeavor allowed me to overcome suspicions that bitter personal baggage would burden the encounter.

We negotiated over a meeting place like two sides to a protracted war. We finally agreed on the boat landing at the village of Sand Creek in northeast Dunn County. It was a site associated with friendlier times and an outing with mutual friends.

Tom kept me waiting past the nine P.M. meeting time. A cruising deputy sheriff twice cast the spotlight of suspicion on my truck. The Big Dippers's reflection flickered on the surface of the Red Cedar River as shooting stars fell into the northern horizon glow from Chetek. Finally, a hour and a half later, another pickup crept into the boat landing parking lot.

Yeah, I'm late. I'm lucky to be here at all. We had a big tussle with the farm credit people down in Pepin County. We had to run old Donny's cattle up to Cornell to hide them on another farm before they were taken away for the debt.

Before we get started, let's clear the air. I know we've had our disagreements. But I'd like to put them aside. We need some advice. There are odd stories circulating about what you're up to. So you tell me if I'm barking up the wrong tree.

Some say you've given up on social justice and that you've gone nuts on some combination of religion and ghost chasing. I don't know what you're doing. But I suspect you've got some sort of angle. I do know that there's some odd stuff starting to happen. Everybody I know from the old networks are edgy. Everybody has a strange story or two they want to whisper so that it doesn't get around that they're seeing things.

So if you have some information that would help us make sense of any of this, you better come across with it. There are lots of people still trying to figure out what to do next. I know it seems like the progressive groups have withered and blown away. Maybe you think they're ghosts, too. Maybe. But maybe some people are still there. Waiting just out of sight, just below the surface. Waiting for...? Maybe for a sign. And maybe we have a sign.

He's back, you know. You know, our hellraising buddy. The one we lost a few summers ago in the tractor rollover. He's making the rounds. I could click off a hundred people who've seen him. A dozen who you know. From Turtle Lake down to Fountain City.

Nobody is calling him by his name. I think we're scared to. Then there's the family to think of. So Big John gave him an appropriate name: Hay River Hellraiser. He's doing much the same thing he did in life. Visiting with individuals to kick their asses and put some fight in them. Leading and inspiring the good guys. Harassing and confusing the bad guys.

A lot of us had our first visits in the middle of the night. He sat on the edge of my bed and woke me up. Gave me what for on everything he thought I'd done wrong in the last two years. Hell, he even shamed a couple people into putting the money back into group treasuries they had "borrowed" it from. You know how it is with money and farm groups. Sticky fingers and poor bookkeeping.

94

Then he started showing up at our events. He grabbed one of those Farmers Home Administration geeks by the necktie. He yelled down a sheriff's auction on the courthouse steps. He even marched with some treehuggers, peaceniks, and Indians up at the Ladysmith mine. There was even an incident at a farm credit office that sure sounded like his work. All sorts of files destroyed. I guess even computer records erased.

All this had the old networks buzzing. The old Finns and ex-Labor and Farm Party people. The Nuclear Freeze and Stop ELF people. The Farm Unity and Farmers Union veterans. At first, only those of us who knew him from his days in Hay River country in Dunn and Barron counties could see him. But after a while, lots of people who never knew him could see him. Old friends from his radical days in ag college heard about it and they came over from Minnesota.

Then stranger things started to happen. Somehow down-on-their-luck country people from all over started to hear about him. Just by word of mouth. And they started to come. At first, just a few from southwest Wisconsin and Iowa. Then they came in caravans. Iowans and Minnesotans mostly, but a fair number of people from the Dakotas and even Ontario and Saskatchewan. All looking for hope.

Some found it. It became sort of like those places in Europe and Mexico where people go for cures and to see statues crying or bleeding. Some went away energized. We heard about others who went home and fought government flunkies and potlicking creditors.

And that wasn't all. It seems that many other dead hellraisers were activated in all this fuss. There's a ghost of a Finnish ore boatman. Another ghost of a two-fisted lumberjack. Another of an Ojibwe World War One hero. The old people told us all these other ghosts had appeared at various times in the past. The thing was they all appeared at times just before something significant happened. They were omens or harbingers.

So the feeling is that between our ghost, the old ghosts, and our pilgrims, something big is going to happen. That's why I wanted to talk to you. If you have any idea about what comes next or what we should do next, then please help us out. If not for me or the others, at least for him.

We want to know. Are we seeing the beginning of a movement? Or the beginning of the millennia? Or simply the stumblings of a new cult? Did we bring him back or is he bringing us back to our senses? Tell us where the Hay River Hellraiser fits in the scheme of things. Let us know whether you're for us or against us.

The Revenirs of Teaching Rocks

M*y Hay River informant issued a warning about my next stop before I left the Sand Creek boat landing. He knew I was headed to the nearby Connorsville area. He was fearful that I would be thrown off track by the source waiting for me at a new community in the town of New Haven. There, nestled in the wooded hills, a group of outsiders sought to create a peaceful space for reflection.*

The warning focused on the other-worldliness of the strangers; on their lack of concern for the struggles of those living in the northwoods. It was a warning deeply infused with the fear of the "other," of those different from ourselves. It was an ironic fear, coming as it did from someone outside what is thought to be the mainstream. It raised my antennae for signals of a "turf" problem.

The warning in no way prepared me for the profound shift I was to find in the relationship between my next source and his ghosts. I thought the references to revenirs and teaching rocks would place me back into a traditional northwoods milieu of French folklore and special magnetism like that of Ouija Board Rock.

Instead, I found an entirely new blend of traditions. It was a different paradigm that called everything that came before it into question. When "Ishmael" told me that he had taken that name as a rebirth, a flash of biblical and literary light flickered in his eye.

🔥 🔥 🔥

We are not here to challenge anyone. We seek only our own path. A chance to meditate and find peace. But the teaching rocks at the headwaters of Flayton Creek demanded our attention. Especially when the Revenirs—as our Creole priestess calls returning spirits—became stronger at the rocks.

Revenirs, she told us, are ghosts consigned to come back to a specific place. Usually it's because violence or evil deeds draw them to a site. But here, it's because the ghosts themselves lose force and come to recharge. They find a synergy here and they learn from each other. You might call teaching rocks a type of ghost seminary and spa.

We have learned much from them. But they did not teach us willingly. We let them into our souls as acts of love. But we found that they don't want us to learn about them because our understanding weakens them. I'll explain.

We have many spiritual currents here at our community. Most find expression in eastern thought. Some involve new combinations of old traditions. A first step here involves honesty about pain. First, get in touch with your own pain. Then with the broader pain. The pure, unadulterated pain of life. This is the step to understanding why we have so many painkillers. That's why we have drugs, booze, cigarettes, shopping malls, casinos, pornography, televised bowling, and psychic hotlines. To dull pain.

The pain is coming right up out of the earth. Riding up on ghosts. It's the pain of millions who have starved. Pain of pogroms, re-education camps, disappearances, death squads, Chernobyls, Bhopals, Sarajevos, Hiroshimas, lynchings, and executions. Not to mention your garden variety serial killers, wife beaters, child molesters, torturers, and so forth. Victims and perpetrators alike. All amplifying.

It's a legacy of pain that goes way back to at least when Cain killed Abel. Maybe back to when God consigned Lucifer to his fallen angel status. Think of the billions of death screams the earth has heard. Starting from the time when we as a species were several links down on the food chain.

Then up to the time when we became advanced enough to form tribes so we could kill each other over things like whose goats got to drink at the water hole first. After that, we got real sophisticated and set up governments so we could kill each other on a grand scale over possession of shiny rocks.

It's not fashionable in these days of don't-worry-be-happy to talk about life as a veil of tears. The power of positive thinking, right? No doubt the universe is unfolding as it should, right? Well, that's what the spirits of pain would have you think. They want you in a stupor.

But the pain isn't the end of it. No, my eavesdropping on the ghost at the teaching rocks taught me that it's fear that makes us cling desperately to the pain. The fear of death that stalks us mercilessly throughout our lives. The fear of grim mortal certainty. The fear that propels all our antlike scurrying, devouring, coupling, and fighting.

This fear is the only reason that there is a market for Volvos, purebred poodles, yachts, and collector art. You might say that the acquisition of wealth is the biggest drug used to fight this fear of death. The assumption is that if we acquire enough stuff we'll forget that we all end up worm chow. It helps us avoid the realization that we'll still be dead a zillion years after our dying sun has swallowed all molecules in the Earth.

But it can't change the inevitable. Acquisition and the pursuit of acquisitions only cut off the possibility of an authentic life in the here and now. There's the pain-fear connection I've seen in the ghosts here. The rich feel the fear. Then they inflict the pain. The response to the pain fuels more fear.

The Marxists were all wrong about material things. That's just playground fighting over toys. The Unabomber is a more accurate expression of the pain-fear connection. That's why we have more ghosts than ever. Contented lives don't generate ghosts. Pain and fear do.

I've been in contact with all sorts of ghosts at the teaching rocks. Many are what you'd expect: crushed loggers, greed-crazed timber barons, and epidemic-claimed pioneer families weakened through malnutrition.

What surprised me were the modern-day ones that pass through the rocks. Odd pairs like debt-ridden farmers who committed suicide and crooked farm credit executives. All sorts of quadruple bypass corporate managers who found themselves downsized. And masses of older workers who lost jobs and benefits at places like Patrick Cudahy, Allis Chalmers, International Harvester, and American Motors.

The lesson they all taught me—without meaning to—is about the awesome sacredness of life. Spirits are eternal. But life is momentary. But because of pain and fear, we miss the point and can't figure out how to live in the here and now.

If we could liberate people from fear and pain it would be a breakthrough. But there are powerful forces to oppose such a breakthrough. The entire economy and political structure as we know it would become irrelevant and would shrivel up. Who would cut an old-growth forest or pollute a stream if they could move past fear and pain into the pure joy of life in the moment? That's the paradox!

The tree huggers think you need to counter short term rich geezer thinking with long-term ecological thinking. If we really understood the marvel of life we would know that short-term and long-term are human conceits. Unless you are a voyeuristic ghost looking in on life, life is NOW.

Life is watching your two-year-old discovering a spider web. It's watching a Down's syndrome child take immense pleasure in simple accomplishments. It's sharing the bounty and beauty of a grandparent's garden. If you can experience those things as fully and consistently as you should, you won't strip-mine coal or build stealth bombers.

So I learned all the stuff of death comes from the hold ghosts have on us. They seem to have an investment in keeping us on their level. It could be that they draw energy from the fear and pain. Maybe they intuitively know that anyone who really lives in the now has the strongest armor against ghosts that exists.

We'll take you there. Just prepare yourself. The grove and rocks are simply magical. But don't be fooled into crediting the ghosts with this feeling. They're really quite boring and petty.

Ghosts of the Peshtigo Fire

M*y journey required that I make yet another west-east traverse of northern Wisconsin. Highway 64 in Connorsville was the logical route to Peshtigo. But it also offered the most lonely five-hour overnight drive I have ever made. The farmland patches of Dunn and Chippewa counties gave way to dark stretches of scrub aspen and twisted stands of jack pine. Medford, Merrill, and Antigo offered no signs of human activity other than electric lights.*

The drive gave ample opportunity to think about the lessons of the revenirs, the hellraiser, the angry dead of Porte des Morts, the herb gatherer, the death guide, the soldiers council, the Lac Vieux canoes, and all the others. Something was stirring. The pieces just didn't fit together. Benign agents of mischief or instruments of dark forces? Weakened remnants of energy or active purveyors of terror and insanity? All of these things?

Perhaps fatigue prevented greater insight on my part. Leaden eyelids and slowed reflexes made the trip hazardous. East of White Lake I started to see the apparitions of all the ghosts I had investigated in the past. One by one they jumped out on the centerline to taunt me and jolt me awake.

East of Langlade, these jolts finally built up enough sense of risk in my tired mind to allow a break for sleep. Maybe the ghosts had saved my life. Forest Road 2118 offered an inviting turn off of Highway 64. I thought it would be a good place to avoid a swooshing semi-truck that might shake me out of slumber.

Sleep was short-lived. The truck rocked and jarred me back to adrenaline-filled wakefulness. A critter or a stalker? A sense of dread filled me. Another symptom of fatigue or intuition?

It was time to move on. I raced down the deserted main drag of Mountain, zoomed past Bagley Rapids, and barreled past the Highway 141 intersection. I did not slow down until I reached the Harmony cutoff to Peshtigo. I did not take a deep breath again until I saw my next contact outside the Badger Paper Mill gate.

An odd odor seemed to waft up from the Peshtigo River. Something from the mill or something from upstream? The lanky fellow poured himself coffee from a thermos. Al's light cotton coveralls caught the glow of dawn's first light.

🔥 🔥 🔥

I don't have long. A guy I know from fishing up at Lac Vieux Desert told me you might be interested in my Dad's experience. It has to do with ghosts of the Peshtigo fire.

My Dad always said that it should have been called the "Great Nicolet Forest Fire." He said to call it the Peshtigo fire made people think only of the town burning, not the fact that it was the worst forest fire in America in terms of loss of life. The whole thing was sort of overshadowed by the Chicago fire. And it has been forgotten that the dry autumn of 1871 was a time of many big fires.

Dad said that everything between the Wolf River and the Peshtigo River was totally burned up with the exception of the Menominee Indian Reservation where they didn't have the pine log slash. And I guess it burned all the way west to Kempster and Elcho and down to Oconto Falls.

There is some reason to believe that it was actually three or four fires that merged together. At least you hear stories of people who took refuge in creeks and saw the fire come at them from both sides. In different locations the fire came from different directions.

When you talk about the death toll, you always hear the phrase "over 800 lives claimed." I would say that the figure of 800 is fairly conservative. Dad always thought it was at least twice that. No one really knew how many people were out in the pine slash.

My Dad was the first one to talk about the Peshtigo Fire ghosts. He took a lot of grief for it. He was considered by some to be a crackpot. For some reason, people around here never liked to talk about the deaths outside Peshtigo. Dad said there were large numbers of hermits, squatters, and nomadic Indians living in the burned territory that were never accounted for. He figured at least three hundred people were in this category.

He even felt that it was possible that land speculators may have intentionally started the fire to clear off the land of other claimants. He said there was once some documentation for this theory at the Peshtigo Fire Museum, but that the evidence disappeared. When he brought attention to the missing documents the local elite mocked him and called him a crank.

He cataloged the ghosts as he discovered them. Plenty of people would talk about them privately. They were pretty much what you would expect. Homesteader ghosts. Logger ghosts. Teamster ghosts. We have those by the dozens.

But there are some rarities. At Wilcox, we have four little girl ghosts—sisters I suppose—in singed nightgowns. At Pound, there's a ghost that appears as a charred body that you can smell. At Coleman, you can see a caravan of burning wagons on the anniversary of the fire. Over by Breed, there are those who have seen a ghostly mirage of a burning Indian village. They say you can hear screams as the bark lodges go up in flames.

At White Potato Lake, there is a ghost of a hermit whose eyes were burned out. He gropes around in the dark trying to find who knows what. If you block his way he'll look up and you will see flames in his eye sockets.

But, in a way, these dozens of human ghosts were not as interesting as the other things he discovered. He found that the fire had unleashed other spirit powers. He didn't even know what to call these.

He found his first one of these near Langlade on Forest Road 2118. Some sort of spirit of a large terrible beast. That one turned out to be something that the fire had activated from underneath Roix Springs. The site was even marked on an old French map.

He told me that the monster would not be deactivated until Roix Springs was again surrounded by old growth forest. As a paper-mill worker, all I can say is, fat chance. He found ghosts of giants and ghosts of mastodons. He found two-hundred-foot white pines that could change locations and hills that have heartbeats.

Despite the ridicule he had to put up with, he felt he was doing important work. He thought that there was nothing more important than discovering the nature of spirits. He thought it was the way to discover important truths abut life. I think he was really getting close to some answers when he died. He's still trying to work on it, I think. His spirit comes to the old house now and then.

He keeps pointing at a wall map there. When I look, his finger is always at the same place: the Menominee Reservation. No way I'm going down there!

Curse From Afar

The lessons of Peshtigo again raised the questions of how the disturbance of nature might be connected to the agitation of spirits and who (or what) might ultimately be responsible for setting off the chain reaction. It was clear that ecological damage was a major part of the equation. Human activity was also a component. But where were the missing puzzle pieces about the timeframes and locations of the initial disturbances?

Clues were abundant. But they pointed in a bewildering variety of directions. Greedy exploiters and trickster spirits. Primeval forces and technological impacts.

The next location that required investigation was an obscure site near Five Islands in the heart of the Menominee Reservation. There, at a hidden encampment, was a source alleged to have made all the stops I had, plus many others. Whispered accounts spoke of a magician and a prophet rolled into one.

Warnings accompanied the whispers. The Five Islands encampment was not a place that an outsider could just drive up to and start asking questions. Several days of phone negotiations were required before I received clearance for a visit. The terms were very specific and very unlike the usual non-committal discussions a stranger often finds on a reservation.

Menominee County's towering white pines loomed like a distant mountain range on the drive up from Shawano on Highway 47/55. On passing the county line, I was enveloped in a dark coolness. At Keshena, the road divided and Highway 55 pulled me northward like a riptide.

A dusty road east of Five Islands led to the encampment. The tree boughs closed in on the truck. The road seemed to disappear. A banging fist on the hood of my truck warned me to stop. Three Menominee men with M-16s blocked the way and motioned for me to get out. A quick walk down a brushy trail brought us to a shack. A large man stepped out of the balsam fir shadows. Wawkaw gave me a hearty greeting.

🌿 🌿 🌿

So we spirit chasers finally meet. Never mind my hospitality associates. We must be careful. There are many enemies of the traditional way of life. Think of the assault rifles as pipes with powerful tobacco.

You want to know why the spirits are acting up and how it got started. Well, I could be a smart-mouth Indian and say that it all started when Ferdinand and Isabel sent Columbus out to pillage and plunder. But I'd only be partly pulling your leg. You know that the Iroquois have a role in this. But there's a lot you don't know about how they fit in and how this place fits in.

First you have to go back into Menominee history. We weren't always good neighbors. Our welcome wagon has often been like the one you got today. We never were as much into the Algonquin brotherhood stuff like the Ojibwe or the Potawatomi. The Winnebago, Potawatomi, and Ojibwe all have stories about how they gave the Menominees gifts of sacred drums and how we failed to treat the drums with proper respect.

The drums have a spirit and should be treated with the same reverence as a grandparent's grave. If you insult the drum or mistreat the drum, you have left yourself wide open for problems. That's what apparently happened to the Menominee who mistreated the gifts from the other tribes.

The problems began when the Dutch in the Hudson Valley armed the Iroquois. This led to the trade wars. The French intervened. The English supplanted the Dutch and kept arming the Iroquois. The Lake Huron and Lake Erie tribes were pushed out to Wisconsin. The new presence of Ottawa, Sauk, Fox, southern Potawatomi, Miami, Mascouten, Kickapoo, Huron, and Petun placed a lot of stress on the environment and disrupted the Menominee seasonal cycle. All because of fashion demands in Paris and London for fur!

The environmental strains led to wars. Wars led to famine and disease. Old alliances—like that with the Winnebago—broke down. The Winnebago stirred up conflicts with the newly arriving tribes. Yet the Menominee paid the price. We shrank down to forty households.

The role of women in all the tribes was debased. We became militarized. Securing furs for trade and fighting wars was now the sole purpose of the tribe. All because of European geo-politics and consumer preferences!

Well, things got bad enough that the Iroquois decided to put a curse on the Ottawa and Potawatomi. So they put their most powerful medicine into an object. The object contained all the most powerful evil spirits of their tradition. So what do the Potawatomi do? Well, they lead this Iroquois war party with this secret weapon right into the heart of Menominee country. That's right, right here is where they left their super spirit H-bomb.

What came next was a time of craziness. The Jesuit missionaries were burned out. Our enemies were then cannibalized instead of just run off. It gave us a bad reputation. But you'll notice we weren't moved to the Skunk Prairie Indian Reservation and Waste Disposal Site in Pisspot, Oklahoma. And we avoided the temptations of Pontiac, Tecumseh, and Black Hawk and their ill-fated uprisings. So it pays to be a little crazy sometimes.

Naturally, you want to know what the deal is on this Iroquois "device." Well, it's more than just a thing that delivers a curse by stirring up spirits. It's also a doomsday device.

We're not about to tell anybody how it works. We'll just let that stew in the clutter of all the end-of-the-world stories. You know, end of millennia and Book of Revelations stuff.

Despite what you've heard, I'm not a wizard or a sorcerer. I laugh at that. I'm not a Jim Jones or David Koresh. This is not a cult. No, this is a warrior research and development site.

This device sets off killers and wackos. It can make even logical people resist the logical steps real humans would take to clean up their own mess. And it teaches us that logic isn't the strong medicine we need. The warrior's job is to block this danger. We sought to destroy it, disarm it, or deflect it. We learned that to attempt the first two things would set off the doomsday feature. The third thing we're still working on.

But now we have our own disagreements about how to use the device. Some actually want to touch off the doomsday feature as our contribution to the Great Cleansing Time. Others want to use it as a secret weapon. Some even want to harness all the cannibalized victim zombies and send them out to stir up more spirits.

We have our own treaty conflicts brewing. We may need the help that the device can provide if we learn to operate it properly. And if we can hold on to it in spite of powerful interests. Think about who might want to harness awesome destructive energy.

Think of the potential to have a whole people commit genocide by themselves. Maybe that's how you do a Cambodia? Then who needs little things like heroin, crack, and AIDS?

Stay focused. Don't get diverted by the Iroquois leads. The old troubles were just a part of those times. The Iroquois today are just like us, trying to get back on track. Don't get diverted by the drum stories. That's just context for the relationships between the tribes. Now we have our own secret drum. We don't need gifts that make us out to be deranged cousins.

Don't even think that there's magic in this place that can help. The magic of Menominee country is no cows and no plows. Our friendly spirits are mostly at Keshena and Neopit. The nastier spirits are mostly outside our boundaries. So if you must visit, visit the Grandmother Spirit on Wayka Creek. Or the Bear Ghost on Red River. Or the Ancient Chief at Big Smoky Falls.

But this is not tourism promotion for us. This is a war and we are getting ready for battle. If you want to survive the Great Cleansing time, I suggest that you get ready too.

Stockbridge's Ohdohs

The question of who (or what) could set off the chain reaction of spirits was still fresh in my mind on my drive to Bowler. The stew of old legends, fear of government conspiracies, and concern over technology run amok and degradation of the environment left a puzzle of enormous proportions. But encounters left me feeling woozy with the contradictions between many of the stories. Not only did I feel inadequate as a detective of the paranormal, I also started to lose my optimism about finding the unifying mythic and folkloric themes behind Northwoods stories.

My Menominee source sent me to the Stockbridge-Munsee Reservation with a benediction and an admonition. He told me I would find some comfort at Bowler. But he also gave me very precise instructions on how to approach my next location without ever identifying a contact. "Empty your mind," he said. "Put aside everything you have heard. Don't ask questions. Just listen and watch. Open your mind and heart to the possibility of more than one truth."

Even my drive was to be a ritual: Offer tobacco at Lower Red Lake, offer sage at the old Gresham mission, and offer cedar on the North Branch of the Embarrass River. Then I was to wait by the water. The wait turned into a long fast. A long, dizzying internal grappling with a lifetime of doubts and fears. One by one, the concerns were dissolved by my hunger and fatigue. When finally I felt like I was going to lose consciousness, Nassahegon stepped out of the hazelnut bushes with a cackle.

🌿 🌿 🌿

Hey white man, I thought you would never get tired. We were testing you. And you were entertaining for awhile—as long as you were picking your nose and scratching your butt. We watched and made bets on when you would leave. But then you went prayerful on us and we had to wait until your collapse.

You are probably too tired to know who we are. I am Chief to the Ohdoh Tribe, and these are my brothers. We deal with one of the Stockbridge ghost tribes. You probably know that the Stockbridge-Munsee are an eastern remnant tribe. And you probably know the connection to the "Last of the Mohicans" story. But you probably did not know that they brought many other small bands with them, like those from Brothertons, Delawares, and Narrangansets.

I am certain that you did not know that the Stockbridge tribe brought the spirit tribes with them too. Yes, you heard me correctly, they brought ghosts such as us from the east coast. Wiped out and extinct tribes like the Conestoga. Tribes that whites never heard of, like the Wanaque, Pohatcong, and Mahantan.

These and dozens more that are not remembered, except here. Tribes that existed for thousands of years and then disappeared in a few seasons. Victims of small pox, cholera, and Iroquois aggression. Their spirits rest here now to await the earth cleansing time.

Two of the ghost tribes are different. Our Ohdoh have been a ghost tribe for ten thousand years. The Nagumwasug at Red Lake have always been a spirit tribe. The Ohdoh went underground during the last time of the Big Ice. When the other tribes moved south, we became spirits. It was then our job to fight evil in the underworld and to deal with spirits hostile to Algonquin people.

The Nagumwasug are a tribe of dwarf spirits. They fight evil spirits of the sky and the waters. They possess very old magic. Together the Ohdoh and the Nagumwasug guard both the living Stockbridge-Munsee and the many ghost tribes and the thousands of natural spirits that fled the eastern cities.

We have three main enemies. Two are Iroquois. One is Chippewa and Menominee cross. All three could harm the Stockbridge-Munsee if we dropped our vigil.

The most numerous are the Chenoo. The Chenoo are Iroquois stone giants who can hide as boulders. They often stalk Indian people who fish near waterfalls. They are the ones who destroyed the old canoes on the rough rivers. The most horrible-looking are the Akaree. They are Iroquois female skeleton spirits. They visit Algonquin men at night and, through magic, seduce them. When morning comes and the men see what is in their beds, they go insane.

The most dangerous are the Chippewa and Menominee Bekuch. It is an extremely strong night spirit. It is probably something their medicine men conjured up to fight Windigos and Wenebojo. But it got out of their control. Much evil in the area between the two big lakes comes from these Bekuch when they move into white men's souls.

The Ohdoh and the Nagumwasug have them under control in Stockbridge country. But it is a constant struggle. And it is made harder by the white men's inventions that disturb nature in ways that make spirits unpredictable, even creating new powers. In our thousands of years of dealing with spirits—fighting the evil ones and protecting the good ones—we have come to understand many things about spirits. Each spirit is a slightly different reality. Each one is a testimony to the Creator's love of diversity.

The spirit has in its energy the code for its life essence. Almost like your white man's science can find in living things in the body's invisible small parts. That essence from the spirit can move into another type of living thing without that creature being haunted.

Look at that eagle above us. In the eagle there is the spirit of a long-ago chief from the ocean where the sun rises. He is here because he is a grandfather to you and the Stockbridge-Munsee. Yes, that is true. Although they will not admit it, many white people with deep roots in this country share Algonquin blood.

When you understand how much we share, you will be able to look at spirits and nature differently. You will hear the birds singing and finally hear the sacred songs of our ancestors. The wind in the pines will reveal itself as the wisdom of the grandfathers.

So take heart. Let these spirits and your guardian spirit—yes, I see him at your side—lend you their courage. By the end of your journey you will have knowledge of hundreds of evil spirits. But remember that the good spirits are as plentiful as the stars in the night sky.

Burning Mission Martyrs

The evolution of my sources, from neutral observers of ghosts, to mediators of spirits, to active agents of ghosts, left me worried about my whole approach to this work. My former folklore/sociological methodology was brushed off by my on-edge, conspiratorial sources. I grew fearful about my ability to maintain my preferred neutral but open-minded stance.

The spirit confidants back at Stockbridge anticipated that I would need to resume my traditional approach after my sojourn with them. They advised me to skip my leads near Gillett and Oconto Falls. They informed me that both sites were simply subsidiary phenomena connected to incidents near Copper Culture State Park. And they let me know that I would find a congenial source.

My trip to Oconto had no eerie or threatening incidents. My mood lightened for the first time since before Washington Island. This time there was no hidden road rendezvous, no dimly lit meeting site, and no indications of ominous forces. Instead, there was warm hospitality at

*the modest home of a writer of religious history who lived on Oconto's
south side. Francis's sense of humor broke the ice.*

※ ※ ※

Welcome to my parlor, said the writer to the guy. Doesn't it figure
that a Protestant fellow—especially one dabbling in pagan elements—would eventually be forced to return to a Catholic source?

You haven't always asked about your sources' religious affiliations,
have you? You younger folks like to celebrate diversity, don't you?
You may celebrate it, but do you understand it? Back in my day, the
brothers and priests at my boys' seminary made sure we understood
who we were. But then the Church has always wrestled with the babel
of the many groups under its umbrella.

You think you want to know about some ghosts at Copper Culture State Park. That's not why you are really here. But I can tell you
that story while we are at it. Yes, there are ghosts out at that site. Old,
old ghosts. Some of the oldest in this part of the state. But they are
weak and fading. Did you know that happens with some spirits?

Sometimes they are like echoes that finally lose their energy. Other
times, a ritual proves their undoing. Like exorcism or when summoned
and used up by black magic. And, as you are also learning, they can
be drained and co-opted by more powerful spirits.

That's the real story here. That's the story of the Burning Mission
Martyrs. That's what you need to hear. "Martyrs" is a misnomer, but
that's what they are called in orthodox circles.

Since the martyrs have become active again, the old copper culture
ghosts are just faint glows along River Road. Just little luminous balls.
The martyrs, on the other hand, have grown robust. They range the
Oconto River from Rush Point on the bay to Oconto Falls. Some even
say that they are knocking on the Menominee's door at Beary Lake.

But I am getting ahead of myself here. First, I need to take you
back over three hundred years. In 1669, Father Allouez began the mission of St. Francis Xavier on the Oconto River. In 1670, an extremely
interesting thing happened there. A Father Louis Andre used his cru-
cifix to induce a run of fish that fed and impressed the Menominee.

The miracle did not make good Catholics out of the Menominee.
But they certainly became wary of the power of the "black robes." It
was always a tense relationship. The Indians just did not trust men who

rejected the comforts of women. Jesuit attempts at interference with polygamy and traditional ceremonies led to resentment.

The simmering bad mood boiled over in the early 1680s when smallpox swept through Green Bay and down the Fox and up the Wolf Rivers. Half or more of the Menominee were killed. Some small bands of Ottawa, Fox, and Potawatomi were entirely wiped out. The Menominee blamed the Jesuits and thought that the "black robes" had put a curse on them for refusing to settle at the mission. "Christianized" mission life interfered with the trapping and fur trading that brought material goods into the area. The French traders fed this animosity toward the missionaries.

In 1684, the epidemic claimed most of the Indians who remained in the vicinity of the mission. The main Menominee bands, along with some surviving stragglers from other tribes, launched a punitive expedition on the mission. They burned the mission. They burned the sick and dying within its crude hospital. They executed the mission's lay workers.

The priests escaped. But most came to rather bad ends in Green Bay shortly after their escape. By 1690, the Wisconsin mission movement was dead and would not be revived for nearly forty years.

What really happened at the Oconto River Mission? It's hard to say. But there is some suggestion that there was some disturbance of a sacred site. Something like what happened at Villa Louis in Prairie du Chien or at the State Capitol in Madison. But that's where this building power of some of the ghosts comes in. Some think that the spirits of the priests came back to the mission. Then they picked up the energy of the other ghosts in the area—including the burned-up ones and the executed ones.

As you might suspect, they are not a positive force. There is pretty much evidence of a vengeful attitude. They have harassed Indians and pagan-leaning whites. I have been told that they disrupt ceremonies.

There is something very troublesome about them. As a modern Catholic, I am embarrassed to say they embody those extremely narrow-minded attitudes that were at the core of the Inquisition. As they grow in strength, they will probably try to bring trial by fire and pain to their adversaries. Just like back in the Inquisition, there is the question of who or what is served by this vengeful mindset. Is it Lucifer or political or economic interests? Is there any difference?

110

The vengeful in spirit can always be bent to dubious causes. Think about the low points in Church history like turning a blind eye to the Nazis or complicity in Cold War atrocities. I am concerned that the forces of orthodoxy will manipulate these spirits and use them as weapons in a new Inquisition. There is plenty to worry about in a time when shooting doctors and bombing clinics are done in God's name.

So, seek out the deeper spiritual truths behind the matter of spirits moving among us. Get to the core of those Indian beliefs and the original brand of Christianity. They have something in common. The connection is in how they use magic and ghosts to talk to their Creator.

Mead Lake's Lost Powwow

The spiritual cross-currents between the original inhabitants and the European boat people were coming into clearer focus with each mile of my journey. But how do I measure them and fit them into the puzzle of the power of the land itself and the imbalance of man's politics and science? That was the cosmic question that ran on a tape loop in my mind as I traveled from Oconto to Mead Lake. The night trip westward on Highway 29 was uneventful except for the occasional deer in the highlights.

But when I turned southward on County M in Thorp, I noticed that a truck which had passed me back in Wausau was about to pass again. This time the occupants were wearing ski masks and the passenger brandished a large handgun. They ran me off the road. Random act or personalized "message?"

The event did give me plenty to think about during a night spent in an abandoned barn outside the hamlet of Willard. Instructions were quite clear that I was to stay put for the night. At sunrise, I made my way to a hilltop southwest of Willard. There, my next guide joined me. He was a large Ojibwe man. He made a cryptic remark about "everyone" having a busy night. He made a few remarks about "preparing" me, shared a light meal, and told me to fast until he came back.

Did the sun come up four times while I waited? Or did hunger cook and eat my brain? I think I was just numb from the near-accident. When Jimmy broke my reverie he looked incredulous and apologetic.

🔥 🔥 🔥

Are you still here? It's been what—couple, three days? I wish I could say that it was a test. You know, we Indians seeing how far you white guys will go. Testing your commitment seeking the spiritual path.

But the explanation is simpler than that. I was called away on a family emergency. Then I just plain forgot about you. Well, after a couple of days I did remember, But I said, "Nah, he wouldn't still be up there."

So you've been here long enough to make contact with spirits. Hell, long enough to make contact with spirits in distant galaxies. So you should be ready to hear what I have to share with you.

It is time for you to learn the power of the powwow. Not the modern tourist powwow, but the ancient "pau-wau." The ceremony of restoring balance. First, you need to hear a story. It's the story of how Cheebeebojo brought pau-wau to the Ojibwe. I'm assuming you know the story of Winona's sons and the special things they brought to the Ojibwe. Well, Cheebeebojo was born to Winona after Pukawiss.

Cheebeebojo was the first of our people to devote his life to exploring the relationships between humans and spirits. Before that, spirits were thought of as things apart, things to be appeased. That attitude—the apartness—crops up in modern man.

He worked out all the basic techniques we use today. I don't mean the aids, like the pipe, the lodge, and the drum. I mean the internal methods. He developed dream communication with spirits. He invented vision quests. He designed the purification ceremonies. He left a legacy of epic verse, song, and music. And he left behind a secret order to preserve the knowledge.

The knowledge is not connected to tribal status. I'm not enrolled anywhere even though I'm over half blood. We recognize all those seeking knowledge. You can know the first part of the knowledge without danger: Cheebeebojo is the principal chief of all the ghosts and main medicine man of the underworld. If you want to know the rest, you must follow my instructions.

I can send you to the lost pau-wau site. The ancient place of Cheebeebojo. We have only recently rediscovered it. The stories pointed to southeast of Spenser, some near Greenwood, and a few around Fairchild. But it turned out to be Mead Lake.

The path I will send you on—if you consent—contains the clues that we sought. You start here on South Mound. You start with the fast. You walk directly to Middle Mound and climb it when the sun is overhead and make an offering. Then you walk directly to North Mound and climb it and watch the sun go down. When the last sunlight hits the narrow middle portion of Mead Lake, you will see a sign which will tell you where to go.

You will then descend North Mound and walk directly to your sign. There you will receive the knowledge. When you are done there, you will be sent to rediscover your own European medicine roots or white powwow.

At Mead Lake, your present questions will be answered. But you will leave with many more. You will spend most of your life answering them.

At Mead Lake, you will look into the face of incredible beauty and revolting ugliness. You will see a oneness of spirits and see it splinter into thousands of ghosts. You will look into a pit of darkness and see incredible light. You will see right to the core of the central question of life, come to know the answer to that question in your soul, and still never be able to put it into words.

You will be looking at Cheebeebojo.

PART IV

Abandoned Fields and Jack Pine Shacks

Plain Spirit

*W**hat** could I possibly learn about the ancient earth spirits of powwow from a European-American in Stratford? The prospect of my next visit filled me with concern about Indian wannabes and New Ager theft of ancient rituals. My concern was softened when I learned that my next teacher was a "plain" woman. She was a member of an anabaptist religious community which adheres to a simple rural lifestyle.*

Few urban dwellers know much about the plain communities that dot the rural landscape in the western and central areas of Wisconsin. Some may have heard of the Amish, but few understand the "old order" versus "new order" distinctions or the Amish relation to the Mennonites, Brethren, and Hutterites.

The new source gave me new insights into these seemingly tranquil communities of faith. There was, I learned, a tension over certain spiritual practices. Indeed, the Stratford woman had recently relocated from another plain community because of controversy over her spiritual and healing activities. Her first request was that I not identify her exact denomination or congregation.

It was a relaxing visit, filled with talk in a sunny kitchen and walks through gardens and pastures. Her mere presence was a form of healing for me. She explained her place in the network of those wrestling with the problems and dislocations of northern Wisconsin. Part of her problem with her church community arose from her openness to dialogue with American Indian spiritual advisers and counterculture back-to-landers.

Her devout beliefs and simple lifeways were not barriers for her, they were a basis for conversation. Emma talked the talk and walked the walk.

You can't make a separation between spirit and healing. Even most ghosts are in need of healing. They're out of balance. They're usually disconnected from God in some way. It's the same with people. I don't think any are born bad or evil. They just get disconnected from the Creator and His Creation.

Maybe I've spent too much time with the Indians and the hippies—like some say—but those people and my people show me that there's a harmony and balance that must be maintained or you will go crazy. I'm called a "braucher" by those who still speak Deitsch, the old German dialect. Those who don't, call me a powwow doctor. It's an old, old way of life and healing. It comes from the Indian and from olden times in Europe.

Healers at one time freely exchanged their knowledge. But that was before the High Church, government, and science stepped in. First, they burned the healers. Now, they fine them or take them to court.

My faith shapes my practice of powwow. I use mostly prayer and touch. But I use some of the old Indian teachings that our people learned from the Conestoga and Lenni Lenape in Pennsylvania and the Shawnee in Ohio. Then there are all the Indian cures in *The Old Herb Doctor* and *The Indian Household Medicine Guide*. Those books explain that powwow is medicine.

Remember, medicine is for man, beast, the spirits, the plants, and maybe the earth itself. A good life is all about healing and living a Christ-like life. What did Christ do? Didn't he heal? Even from death? Didn't he cast out demons? Didn't he transform things? Didn't he ease hunger and thirst for multitudes? Didn't he comfort the sick, the poor, and the scorned? Doesn't that sound like healing?

But modern people want it both ways. They don't want to give up anything. They want spiritual peace and all their modern conveniences. Yet every valid prophet, teacher, and healer has already told them that it doesn't work that way. There's only one way to spiritual peace: that through avoiding the poison of wanting and needing things. Getting past the material desires is a big challenge. Even for ghosts.

That's right. Many ghosts are locked into their traps because they could not separate from material things. So, often they are stuck close to their property or hidden money or left trying to recapture some pleasure of the material world.

By now you understand that I work with many people in dealing with troublesome spirits. Our friends in Oconto and Mead Lake are a few. We have different ways and there is no one right way.

Many of the people you have met along your journey want you to act like a soldier. It's not that simple. It's true that vigilance and courage are needed. But do not let hatred or fear control you. Study the lives of Saint Sophia and Hildegard of Bingen. Learn how women took care

118

of healing in olden times. Then look at what happened when they burned the women and the plagues came.

I'm working on a Marathon County ghost case right now that might interest you. It was responsible for some barn fires. But we have that part solved. You might say I've been counseling the ghost. It's of a young man who burned barns when he was alive. He was an illegitimate child. He sought revenge on an unknown father. And the barns were the symbols of the inheritance he never received. Healing him will be my next project.

But you see, if someone doesn't attend to these tortured ghosts, they can become bigger problems. I don't know how that works, but I know you've met some people who have some ideas. It's almost as if a ghost can be corrupted in the same way an idle young person can.

And there's so much odd stuff going on. The destruction of community. There's not much left outside our plain groups. No sense of belonging. No sense of stability for children.

Then there are the poisons in the air, water, and food. The new diseases. When you let life's essentials turn bad, you will not only get sick in the body, you will see sickness of mind. Look at AIDS and our blood. Look at all the crazy murderers draining blood. It's the new plague and the new vampires.

And through all of this, fear of death is increasing. Fear of death is causing a fear of real life. That's why so many are frantic and confused. A real reverence for life includes an appreciation of death. Death is grim in many ways. But it cannot be dressed up by looking the other way or covering it up with expensive rituals.

Bury your own dead. Make their coffins. The community should be part of each step. Love and comfort should come from friends and family, not hired embalmers. Something special happens when you take care of your own dead. Others take over the day-to-day things. The chores are done. The animals are taken care of. Messages go out to distant relatives. Big meals are cooked. All as if by magic. The community is the magic.

This way, the mourning survivors can do what they need to do. The release of crying with those close to you builds the bonds of trust and support. The presence of children at every stage helps them understand the finality of death, the celebration of a life that is now over and given over to another stage.

You've probably never heard of a haunted plain community. This attitude toward living and dying is the reason. If you live in a

119

community where you see that love in life and know that's how you will be treated in death, well, there's no reason to hang on as a ghost.

You make spirits tranquil by living a tranquil life. For us, the tranquil life is a plain life. Maybe it can be done other ways. But our way has fewer temptations and complications. In a nutshell, plain living makes tortured ghosts into plain spirits.

Polonia's Polutnitsha

Looking back at my various sources, it was apparent that many had been drawn deeply into the fears and suspicions caused by their experiences and could no longer separate themselves from those emotions. Instinct told me that passion on these matters was definitely the enemy of clear thinking.

As the reports of new incidents and phenomena found their way to my ears, I reminded myself again and again how this search began. It was hard to believe that there had ever been any light-hearted ghost chasing motivation to my travels. It was hard to remember to use the psychological, ethnographic, and folkloric analysis tools that I had acquired.

Thus, it was a relief to find that Portage County was next on my list. Two decades of travel around the state created a fondness for Stevens Point and the surrounding small communities. Whether it be checking out the new tap beers at Witz End tavern, fishing Lake DuBay, or pigging out at the American Legion Friday night fish fry, Portage County became, for me, a symbolic as well as geographic center of Wisconsin.

A source was to tell me about one of those simple Old Country ghosts that always caught my fancy. Andy, a Polish-American potato farmer, sat me down in a root cellar overlooking the Tomorrow River. He let me know there was a twist that fit in with what I was hearing elsewhere.

120

What the dairy farmer is to most of Wisconsin, the potato farmer is to Portage County. So there's lots of stories out there. German, Norwegian, and Irish. Of course, I'm fond of the Polish ones. Especially the ones about Poles and potatoes. The lowly potato was the center of life around here for four generations. It paid off lots of mortgages and sent some youngsters to college.

We had priests blessing the potatoes. We had holidays from school to help with the harvest that we called potato vacation. We all had our cherished potato buckets and our potato forks. Why not a potato ghost?

I'm not an expert on hauntings. The only ghost stories I've ever heard are the ones about the haunted Upham mansion in Marshfield, the haunted Scott mansion in Merrill, and our local potato ghost. When I was a little shaver we heard about the ghosts in the potato barns. It seemed like every potato barn had one. Or, I should say it seemed like every potato barn cellar had a ghost.

Potato barns are less common these days. They're smaller than a dairy barn. They have a haymow drive in the floor with a centered trapdoor. The trapdoor goes to the cellar. That's where the potatoes go. The cellars are heated to keep the potatoes from freezing.

It turns out there is not a different ghost for each potato barn. Nope, it's the same one making the rounds, checking on the crop, and checking on the farmers and their families. I learned that our ghost is a Polish *polutnitsha*. That's a special ghost that guards food crops. It's in a whole category of old European harvest ghosts. In Russia there were the green-bearded *polaviks*, in Finland the rye-dogs, and in Ukraine, the wheat wolf.

All these spirits were set in place by divine intervention. That's why you have things like the story of the goddess Demeter giving mankind the gift of grain. That's why the Chippewa talk of the wild rice coming from the Great Spirit. It's hard to sort out the different cultural parts of the polutnitsha. How did it get to Portage County? How did it get hooked up to the potato crop?

Back in Poland the old polutnitsha was entirely an ancient outdoor tradition. They were in groups of three or more guarding fields. We're talking fields of bread grain, since there were no potatoes in Poland until the last couple hundred years. Old-time polutnitsha spirits were gold-haired women who guarded the fields and kept out intruders and punished lazy farmers.

But it gets more complicated than that. One polutnitsha must have attached herself to the potato crop in Poland. Then she must have hitched a ride to America with the Polish immigrants. There's significance to that circle trip of the potato and to the added-on power of the spirit, if you think about it. It's bound to create new, unpredictable mixtures.

Then you throw in the new elements and technology. You get a mutated old crone that moves around. Makes you wonder what we're putting into the ground, into the food chain, and even into our ghosts.

I think the polutnitsha was transformed by chemicals and stands as a warning. I think she was poisoned by aldicarb, mutilated by herbicides, made half-mad by mercury from power plant fly-ash, and mutated by paper mill PCBs. So she's a survivor and a victim.

Some have been chased away from spray tanks by her. Children have been told by her not to drink from contaminated wells. She guided a friend of mine to some leaking chemical barrels in an abandoned shed. A few years ago she even helped break up an illegal toxic dumping ring. She haunted one of the dumpers so bad that he turned himself and his partners in. Some big fines and jail time on that one.

I've seen her right here in the Tomorrow River country. She pointed the way to a fish-kill that I then reported. I've seen her fly like a witch, only on a spray tank instead of a broom. I've seen her sit right here in this root cellar and scratch at sores on her face. She only says one word over and over: POISON!

The Highground

Sacred spaces and sacred places are part of the journey to the world of spirits. The tribal traditionalists know that well and often build the sweat lodges and teaching lodges in locations that facilitate access to worlds beyond this one. As for European-Americans, well, we are often up the creek without a paddle. Our willingness to commercialize even that which touches our souls is damaging to our inner beings. We are selling our mother.

Our religions offer glimpses of it in the beautiful simplicity of isolated hilltop churches and chapels in wooded glens. But, increasingly, our churches mirror our malls and shopping centers. The Great Spirit speaks not of parking lots.

Public sacred space and sacred place is even harder to find. Public space is ruthlessly secularized to insure that no glimmer of spirit rears its head. All that is profound and touches the soul is banished from our public temples in the name of separation of church and state. Oddly enough, this cleansing serves to devalue the very civic virtues that protect genuine separation.

Our government buildings, our museums, and our parks are left only with their physical grandeur. Their spirits have been exorcised and await conjuring revival. Occasionally a monument or cemetery hints at faded spirits. This especially is true of war memorials and veterans cemeteries. The spirits of sacrifice and suffering are under bronze and granite odes to abstract heroism and behind the inscribed political exhortations to believe that each war is a "just war."

Places which permit that admitting of pain, which is the beginning of the recovery of self, are rare. But there are beginnings, and northern Wisconsin has one such powerful place. Near Neillsville, off Highway 10, there is a sacred place and sacred space dedicated to this recovery. It is called The Highground. It is a memorial to the interlocking Indochina conflicts referred to more simply as Vietnam. There almost always is someone there who understands the journey of recovery.

On the day I drove over from Polonia it was a fiftyish man in a wheelchair who knew the spirits well. Mel beamed the smile of someone who had made the journey back from pain.

🌾 🌾 🌾

Magical things happen in this place. The Highground has turned out to be magic in ways no one ever anticipated. Many of us have seen miracles here. Five years ago I didn't believe in anything. As far as I was concerned, I died the day I lost my legs. It was only a matter of how much booze and dope it would take to finish the job.

Now I know that my adult life began when I stepped on that mine in the Mekong Delta. It was a journey that had to take me through this place. You can call it God, Yahweh, Allah, Shiva, the Great Spirit, or the Great Turnip. But it showed itself to me in this place and now I can see it everywhere.

You don't even have enough time for me to tell about all the lives this place has touched—the lives it's saved. I'll just give you a couple of accounts. Hopefully enough to show what's going on here. The first one I heard about was before I went through my change. At that point, this place was only a way of me saying "look at what happened to me."

Then I met Ron the morning after he slept nestled in the wing of the dove effigy mound. He used to be one mean mother. But he came up from that mound covered with dew and told me that an angel visited him. He said he couldn't say whether it was a dream or not. But he was quite clear about the message. The angel told him to go home and love his wife, to give her a child, and to love that child deeply. The angel promised that if the child was loved deeply that the ghosts of Vietnam would gradually leave him alone. Almost six years later it seems like it worked.

A year later came Damon. By then I had heard a lot, so I was ready for everything. He slept in the dove's wing too. But no angels for him. No, he had ghosts to say goodbye to. He was a sole survivor of a 173rd Airborne Brigade patrol. His buddies bedded down with him right at the mound like they did their last night in the bush. They let him know that their deaths weren't his fault and he shouldn't feel guilty for surviving.

The Indian vets started coming too. We started to have the pow-wows here. They taught me a lot about the specialness of place. There's magic in this spot. There's the vista looking out on an incredible earth. There's the mound made sacred by blood and tears. The chimes that are the bones of our lost brothers. The flowering star, the meditation stone, the powwow circle, and so forth. No cathedral compares to it.

But I was not touched directly yet. I was still like someone waiting patiently at the tent revival. I hadn't personally heard the call to dance down the aisle and get saved. I was just glad to bask in the reflective energy of those miracles. I had to get ready. I guess I was a harder nut to crack. I guess I was feeling pain and anger on so many different levels. But the spirits let me know just how many kinds and how vast a store of pain there was and is.

This place is a magnet for such spirits. Come one, come all. Vietnam vets got ghosts up the wazoo. We whack 'em and stack 'em or whack it and jack it. Take your pick.

I've seen the covert insertion teams from Cambodia and Laos that never came back. I've seen the bones of the pilots resting at the bottom

124

of the South China Sea. I've seen the overdosed heroin addicts turning into fly food in Cholon's back alleys. Hail, hail, the gang's all here.

The hill tribesman abandoned by the CIA—they're here. The kids run over by supply trucks—yup, them too. Greedy whores strangled in filthy beds—check. The prisoners shot or tortured to death by both sides—check. The young bargirls executed by the V.C. as a message not to consort with G.I.s—check. All the old people, women, and children from all the My Lais of all the sides—check, check, check.

I have a hunch that you could even contact peace movement ghosts here. I use to hate those people, but the Highground has gotten me past that. It was really just minorities on either side of the issue who felt entirely certain about what they were doing. The rest of us schleps just went where we were told. To the induction center or the protest march, depending on where our lives placed us.

But those former protesters need to come here too. They need to meet those spirits of Kent State, Jackson State, the Weather Underground, and the vets who were against the war and died in prisons or alone in their own attics.

All wars have this legacy of pain. But here's something different about ours—especially here in Wisconsin where there was so much public reaction against the war. It's even in the language. We say we were "in" Vietnam. Vets from others wars don't say "in" Germany or "in" Tarawa. We say "in" Vietnam like it was an altered state of consciousness or a prison. Maybe it was both.

For some it still is a prison. They need to come here to start the amnesty process for themselves. For those for whom it is an altered state of consciousness there is a different problem. They'll need to deal directly with those spirits here.

Vets see visions and hear voices here. But it's meant to be that way here. One guy—a lifer, still in the military—said he had a vision about how violence had actually altered the earth's magnetic field. He said the vision told him that we can't even afford to have one high atmospheric nuclear explosion. Something about the electro-magnetic pulse destroying the whole planet.

Other guys told me a North Vietnamese vet visited the place and had a vision of building a mound in Vietnam outside Hanoi. And they did. Now they're working on one for My Lai. It's the place to let go of pain. The place where the healing begins. It all begins with the ghosts.

You have to allow yourself to see them again. Despite the horror. Face the maimed, the dying, and the piles of dead. You have to love them, embrace them. It's only after that embrace of the dead that you can feel alive again. That's the healing spirit.

Esprit Embrouille
(Mixed Up Ghosts)

Highground's lessons of ghost mobility, trans-cultural meaning, and spiritual healing built my confidence about this journey through the North Country. It was not just a matter of malignant spirits and spreading contamination. It was also more than wistful wisps. It was an emerging picture of northern Wisconsin: diverse, turbulent, and fecund.

With the sun rising, I was on the last leg of the trip, going to the Town of Hobart. There along Duck Creek, hidden among a cluster of big new houses, is a modest bungalow. As my pickup eased down the dirt lane the smell of fresh coffee and sizzling bacon reached my nose. The lady of the house waved me inside and ushered me to the kitchen table. There, her husband sat in his underwear. The three of us drank and ate in silence.

After breakfast we started into our discussion. Edgar was a retired paperworker, a dark-skinned French-Potawatomi, and an uncommunicative disabled veteran. Beatrice was of Oneida-Mohican-English background, an Oneida tribal employee. Her sunny disposition shone from her startling blue eyes. The talk of ghosts drifted in and out of the terrain of race and ethnicity. It was yet another indication of how Wisconsin's American Indian tribes and early European-American settlers influenced each other.

The story I had come to hear was about a priest and a clan leader who had taken each other's place in the spirit world. But it turned out to be more complicated than that. It was as complicated and as ironic as the personal situation of the couple sitting at that stained enamel table.

Beatrice was the primary narrator. Edgar confirmed by grunts, conceded by shrugs, and added emphasis with wide eyes. Beatrice's staccato delivery underscored the sub-stories and the role division within the marriage.

🌿 🌿 🌿

I'm a talker, no doubt about it. Got that from my mother. But there's also the old Iroquois ways. We were matriarchal, you know. The women picked the chiefs and gave advice. Edgar will tell you I'm full of advice, right Edgar?

You're here to learn about the mixed up ghosts, aren't you? That's quite a tale. Or should I say it's a tail that wags a bigger story. In Edgar's family they called the ghosts the *esprit embrouille*. That's French for confused spirits. There was an old pidgin Potawatomi word for the same thing, but he forgot. Right, Edgar?

I depend on Edgar to fill me in on the Wisconsin Indian stuff. As you can see, I pass for white all the time even though I'm enrolled Oneida. And Edgar looks Indian enough to be in *Dances with Wolves*. But somewhere along the line his people didn't come out of the woods to sign the roll. So according to Uncle Sam, and the Oneida Nation we're an interracial couple.

Our situation has a lot of similarities with these mixed up ghosts. At least in the sense that confusion and mistakes lead to long-term consequences that we can't easily undo. And maybe a little lesson about learning to live with and laugh about those human errors. Right, Edgar?

This all starts back in Old LaBaye during the time of the French. In a hard winter an epidemic swept through and claimed some victims. Two victims were prominent. One was a priest and the other was a local clan leader. Probably Winnebago. With the ground froze you can't bury a body, so the corpses were wrapped or boxed above ground until spring. The two dignitaries were wrapped in black cloth and stored under the trading post floor.

In the spring, the replacement priest directed that the bodies be put in their final resting places. Somehow the bodies of the priest and the clan leader were mixed up. The priest was buried in what later became the old Fort Howard Indian plot. The clan leader was buried in consecrated ground near the East River.

Nobody figured out what happened until later on. That was after the ghosts got cooking in both places. Between epidemics, wars, and fur trading competition, the place was in turmoil even without the ghosts. You had different tribes pushing through. So even when a medicine man identified the problem it was unclear who should correct it. When the English took over they could of cared less. Later with the Americans, it was just a story to be told while boozing on cold winter evenings.

The early stories talked about ghosts who looked lost and sad. Mostly hanging around right where they were buried. But that changed over time and I guess the other spirits in both those burial grounds had something to do with it. By that I mean both souls eventually took on some of the characteristics of the spirits surrounding them. So the priest's ghost started acting a bit Indian and the clan leader's ghost started acting a little European.

Then they started traveling back and forth between the burial grounds, paying each other visits. Finally they started to roam around together. That's when the next phase of this ghost thing got started. Wouldn't you say so, Edgar?

A group of ghosts started to make a circuit with the priest and the clan leader. They all seemed a bit confused. But that was to be expected. Victims of alcoholism, gambling fights, and trading disputes. Offspring from soldier and trader assaults on Indian women. Remnant tribal people dying alone. Dumb European immigrants unprepared for Wisconsin winters. Half-breeds, quarter-breeds, and don't-know-breeds.

So they started to wander the area. They danced on the hilly Oneida graveyards. They splashed up and down Duck Creek. Sometimes they ran in the median of Highway 41. Other times carousing on County J or County E out into Outagamie County. Good Lord, even on the runway at Austin Straubel Airport in Green Bay. Even at the casino and hotel, and in Packer shirts at Lambeau Field.

Lots of different ghosts. Edgar knows the French names but forgot the Indian names. There are the naughty girl ghosts, the *ame* and the *ombre*. There's the *esprit d'chevalier* or warrior ghost. There are the haunting types: the fantome, the revenant, the lutin, and the goule. And there's what we call a celebrating ghost: *esprit d'tapage*.

Edgar says that these common ghosts are derived from mortal souls and left on their own they rarely cause any real trouble. Edgar says the real trouble comes when immortal spirits come into play. There is the *esprit fourbe* or trickster ghost. There is an *esprit malfaisant* or evil spirit. And, most important, the Great Spirit or le Saint-Esprit.

Wherever there are groups of common ghosts the three immortal ghosts come into play. They fight to control the spiritual energy of the group. When the evil spirit has the upper hand then things go bad. That's where the differences between people turn from a thing of wonder to a point of hatred.

On the other hand, when the Great Spirit has the upper hand there is peace and harmony. The living are happy and the ghosts are at rest.

But there's a big gray area in between. The confused area where the ghosts and the living are mixed up. That's the area where the esprit fourbe has the upper hand. This trickster is well known in Wisconsin. He has many names. He is at the center of the strange things that go on among Indians and between Indians and whites. And he's in all of us who are a little bit of both.

The good news is that trickster, the mixed up ghosts, and their merry band of spirits keep the really bad things at bay. For example, the scary things that used to bother the Oneida. The *chenoo* or stone giants, the fearsome *hino* of storms, and the *ga-oh* of great winds are gentler here compared to our old homelands. But the bad news is that the trickster and his flunky ghosts keep us confused. So we end up thinking white when we need to think Indian and thinking Indian when thinking white would lead to a better result. Right, Edgar?

That's where race-thinking and worrying about fractional ethnic heritage come from. That didn't come from Indian-thinking. That's why Indian-thinking causes such ambivalence toward churches, boarding schools, missionaries, and other authorities. The irony of the blood quantum silliness makes me laugh until I hurt. Race has no basis in science. It's all just body features and pigment differences found in lesser or greater degrees in all groups.

The purists on all sides forget some basic things. Mixed-blood people have greater immunity. Don't forget that the main purpose of crossbreeding in animal husbandry is hybrid vigor.

Look what happens to inbred populations over time. The decline in intelligence and strength. Without the crossing of blood there is no long-range survival. That is the lesson of the mixed-up ghosts. That is why the trickster is along the path of survival. Don't you agree, Edgar?

Fire Specter of Black River Falls

While the mixed-up ghosts of the Green Bay area taught me something of spirits within genetic material, there was plenty of reason to believe that forces within the earth had also molded the supernatural environment of northern Wisconsin. My next stop involved a legend about "fire within a hill" and anecdotes about a "fire specter."

The next stop did not come for weeks after my Green Bay visit. So my weeks of crisscrossing Wisconsin on late-night runs came to a temporary halt. When I next resumed my map tracing, I was on a business trip in Stevens Point. Although the respite was welcome, the delay was not voluntary. My original source for Black River Falls was found floating in the lower Black River, the victim of a "boating accident."

Several weeks passed before the network I had come to rely on found an alternate informant. When they finally did, the referral came with many reservations and warnings. They all agreed that I should talk to Sissy. But their comments certainly did not inspire confidence: her mind is going, she denies her Indian heritage one day and flaunts it the next, she is cranky, she hates white men, and she is really a witch.

All these comments brewed in my head as I hit Highway 54 in Plover and diluted as I headed west on a sunny afternoon. The distractions of the pleasant drive almost made me miss the turn onto Cherokee Drive and my destination: The Rainbow Club. But the gritty reality of the revving engines of a line of motorcycles, large primer-painted sedans, and rusty pickup trucks snapped me back into focus. Why was that rough crowd leaving the Rainbow Club? Why was I going into it? It turned out Sissy was the answer to both questions.

As I stepped into the gloom, the jukebox blared Johnny Cash's "Ring of Fire" and broken glass crunched under foot. She was waving what looked like a .25 automatic and screaming about "damn cheaters." I thought she might have been pretty, several thousand cartons of cigarettes and shots of whiskey ago. She wheeled in my direction and growled, "Watchya looking at?"

Madness or inspiration put strange words into my mouth. I told her that a tough gal like her deserved better than such a little sissy gun. I told her that I would be glad to honor her ladylike demeanor

with a couple of shots of her favorite poison. And I confessed my iden-
tity and mission.

"I'm in the mood for a man like you," came the girlish giggle.
"Strong, white, and blubbery that is. Well, pull up a stool, Moby Dick."

Close up, Sissy had all the fragrance of an ashtray and a bar rag.
She leaned my way and I experienced the dual terror of the possibil-
ities of a kiss or vomit. She upped the ante by bringing the gun up
between our faces. She pulled the trigger: Swoosh. It was a cigarette
lighter, not a real gun. She laughed again.

🌿 🌿 🌿

You're playing with fire. But you know that already, don't you?
Fire is hard to tame, hard to understand. It can be tricky when you're
burning brush. It's even trickier when it's burning down in your
pants. You want to know about the fire specter, right? That's a twit
name. Specter, pecker! I just call him the flamer or the flaming you-
know-what.

The old duffers, the ones still following the medicine mumbo-
jumbo, talked about the gift of the spirits. They said that fire came down
to earth from the fighting between spirits. I guess the first man on a
hilltop who raised his stick in the storm got quite a surge of spirit.

But that's what you'd call the good fire, the fire that's a gift from
above. The other fire comes from below. That's the bad fire and that's
where the fire specter comes from. That flamer is an errand boy from
hell. He's the s.o.b. behind every stove burn, brain-frying fever, hunting shack fire, and burnt-out car around here. He's the fire in the blood
that makes a nice fella all of a sudden break a cue stick over the head
of his buddy. He's the boiling stuff in the belly that gets a gal hot for
a no-good skunk of a man.

This is no ordinary hooting and hollering ghost. It's a ghost under
a deep curse. A curse put there by wizards and devils. A curse that
pulls hellfire right up out of the guts of the earth and gives the soul a
scorching enema. That's what the old duffers say.

How did the ghost end up like this? That's the sixty-four-frigging
thousand dollar question. I heard the answer when I was a little girl
while eavesdropping on my grandfather. He and his buddies was
sucking on cheap wine in paper bags and talking about getting over
on white men.

Grandfather was kind of a black sheep in the family. He had married a Jewish woman up in the Twin Cities. Ever since we've been called "Winnebagels." Not a lot of respect from either bunch. Anyway, they talked about a murder up on Bell Mound. A bunch of skins saw a fire up there. They thought a white guy was messing with a sacred place. So they went up there at night to rough him up. Things got out of hand and they killed him.

But that's when the evil started to percolate. They burned up the body and put a curse on it. But they later discovered they had burned up a half-breed eastern Indian. Worse yet, it was a medicine man who was on a visit to the underworld while in a trance. So the local skins did the devil's work. Talk about doubled-up curses and bad things bouncing back on you!

Our ghost didn't get full of fire and vinegar all at once. It's more like a big kettle. It built up or cooled off depending on how the fuel and draft were adjusted. Back in the Great Depression there were people who burned up in the old jalopies they were living in. Then in the 1950s there were all those trailer fires. Later, it was a mix of things like bars, barns, supper clubs, and junkyards. The ghost set them all.

But the big blowout came in 1977. That was the year of the big fire. The year it hit the crowns of the white and jack pines and just raced right through the area. That would not have happened in the old forest when we had the six-foot-thick, three-hundred-year-old pines. So even the big fire was probably a payback for earlier bad stuff.

My boyfriend in those days was a railroad freight car man, someone who fixes train equipment. Mister Goodwrench said that the main causes of those big fires were hot boxes on the trains. You know, axle bearing fires that throw sparks along the tracks. I can tell you from personal experience, that man knew how to fix a hot box.

But he didn't know much about fires or ghosts. He would bring marshmallows to the sacred fire. And when I would talk about spirits he would grab me from behind and ask me if I wanted to get filled with the holy spirit.

You won't find anyone else who will talk to you about this. Most of the old guys are dead and the ones still around aren't big on talking to snoopy white boys. But I can tell you what I've seen and heard. The ghost is still out there. Damn straight.

My uncle saw him as a blue flame shaped like a man. Many of the old duffers saw him as ball lighting rolling down paths on cloudless nights. One old boy even saw the fire spook turn from flame into a big rock and then after awhile turn molten and run down a crack in the ground.

My experiences are a bit different. I've seen the blue flame man, but running up on powerlines. Then I've seen a glowing figure up on top of dead trees...like, whatchacallit, like St. Elmo's Fire. From up on Bell Mound, I've seen the ghost split into many little fires. I call them lost-soul fires.

The strangest thing I've seen is when he's in a campfire. It happens a lot along the Black River from Lake Arbutus down to Irving. It seems like he comes out of driftwood fires when people are fishing at night. Some think it takes a certain kind of driftwood, maybe old wood from the original forest that was clearcut.

The thing that is strange about it is how he looks in those fires. It's a lewd look. Kind of a joker's face with a flame tongue licking in and out. Licking and flicking like he wants a taste of something live. And you're almost tempted to let it happen, 'cause the heat is pulling at you, and yet you know you'll get burned bad.

I think that some others, weaker ones, just let it happen. That fire just hypnotizes them. And he just draws them right in. That's the real fuel here, those souls feed him.

What nobody seems to understand is where he disappears to. Sometimes he's gone for a year or two. Then all of a sudden he's back setting fires and turning up the heat. It's all too complicated for me, what with global warming and all these volcano things going off around the world.

But I have an idea if you want to follow it up on your own. I think he goes down to hell in a hole out at the old Jackson County iron mine. I think he takes souls down that hole and brings back fire. It's just a hunch. It's got to have something to do with what happened to the earth here, the mine, and the cutting of the old trees. That and the back-road vengeance, the beatings, and the strangers buried in the marshes.

You can look for that hole if you want. Or you can wait for him along the river. Or you can come back to my trailer. What scares you least?

Plainfield's Chopper

Highway 54 pulled me eastward again until the Wisconsin River Valley papermills came into sight. At Nekoosa Junction, Sissy's aroma finally left my nose. It was time to head down Highway 73 toward the next stop: Plainfield. After a lull in my visits I intended to complete two stops in one day. The truth was that I was anxious to get Plainfield behind me. It was the one stop that was haunting me years before this northwoods journey was begun.

Perhaps it was the joke that a co-worker had pulled on me twenty years before in having me camp, unknowingly, on the Gein family farm. Maybe it was the sullen responses that I had received every time I had asked Plainfield residents about the horrible crime. It just could have been that something was profoundly out of sync in the area.

By the time I hit the Highway 73 turn at Nekoosa Junction, I was reconciled to my next visit, still chuckling at my last encounter. A faint band of red horizon put a temporary glow in my rear view mirror. It was a friendly and life-affirming end to the day.

My next informant was not an irreverent bundle of energy like Sissy. No, she was literally at the end of a quiet life. Althea was brought home to Plainfield to die. Her cancer was perhaps the only reason she consented to an interview. This deviation from the tight-lipped Plainfield norm scared her even in her dire condition. But her special knowledge infused her with a sense of responsibility.

Like so many of the spirits I had investigated, here there were layers in the local stories. Older and, perhaps, more disturbing tales often provided the foundation for contemporary experiences. Althea's frail voice provided more than a foundation; hers was a revelation of the long suppressed traumas that had silenced a community.

It was a glimmer of an answer to the forty-year-old question of what ever got into Ed Gein.

🌿 🌿 🌿

My body is failing. But I think my mind is still working—more or less. At least I remember things. The dates. The people.

If you were to ask local people when things went wrong, they'd say November 16, 1957 was the day Plainfield came under the cloud.

That was the day little Eddie—that's what I called Mister Gein—went far enough over the edge to get caught.

Everyone will tell you it was the first day of deer season, as if that explains it. I think it just made it stand out in people's minds. The day doesn't explain the actions—or the many horrible things that preceded it—but it does explain the response. The town being empty, except for the women. The slow response of the police. The whisperings about deer meat.

Many people went to their graves thinking about the "deer meat" little Eddie had given them. They tried to remember if the meat tasted like venison. They tried to remember if the gifts were close in time to the disappearance of some of the tavern women. There were dozens of people who had years and years of stomach and digestive problems. That's where my cancer is.

Back then, Plainfield was a village of six hundred. On the surface, it was pretty much like any small town. It had experienced some bad things in its past. But there was still hope for the future. Call it healing or hiding, but very few people knew anything about prior problems. Even after the Gein tragedy there was no acknowledgment of anything deeper.

Plainfield was simply in shock. Absolute, tail-between-the-legs and dark-denial shock. The community changed, trust ended, and a deep dislike of outsiders set in. It was almost as if people thought that if only the outside world would ignore the Gein horrors, then everything would be fine. Maybe they thought that because of other dark incidents in the past that were forgotten.

What is that past exactly? That, young man, is a tricky question. It's a mix of story and fact, suspicion and imagination, fear and guilt. On one side of the ledger you have an old German ghost story. On the other side you have a brutal pioneer occurrence that set a very negative tone for the community.

The ghost story is about der Hacker. That's German for "the chopper." He's a ghost of a woodchopper, a mangled spirit carrying an axe. He is thought to have chopped up others and been chopped up himself. He is seen headless at times, missing an arm at other times, and, on rare occasion, with an axe embedded in his head.

He is a haunting presence, an omen of impending tragedy, and an incitement to murderous revenge. Or so the story has it. I've never seen him. I never heard a firsthand account. It's always what the "old people say" or "somebody said." It's amazing how a story can stay alive without anybody taking any ownership of it. But it's clearly associated with places throughout the towns of Plainfield and Oasis, including the Gein homestead site.

It's something the immigrants brought with them. Not just the story, but the presence too. Somehow the spirit crossed the ocean with the people. Did you ever hear of such a thing? Then there's the gruesome history. In 1853—with the first houses barely built—a settler named Cartwright was lynched at the Plainfield tavern. Not just lynched, but dragged behind a sleigh afterward and the body thrown through the door of his house at the feet of his wife and children.

It touched off a frenzy of violence. Three other people were killed before the next day. All in an obscure land dispute. Some believe that the land in question was out at the Gein homestead.

This all came down to little Eddie. There was something out in those woods that got into him and something here in the village that set him off. In 1944, his brother died in a suspicious marsh fire. That was probably Eddie's first murder. Then in the early 1950s he took some trips in central and western Wisconsin. Years later it was pieced together that young women died and disappeared in those areas.

Little Eddie then switched his attentions over to the old tavern ladies. That's when those murders started. That's also when he started to dig up women's bodies and cut them up. He used skin and body parts to make himself a sick costume. I'd say the chopper took over his body and soul at that point. And the chopper stayed in little Eddie until his arrest on Palm Sunday of 1958 and the spirit burned down the Gein homestead and its secrets.

Body parts were scattered all over western Waushara County. I think they're like seeds of the chopper. They're in our water, our food chain, and even our Christmas trees. It's a human and ghostly compost.

We're still angry at outsiders. But it's really more about our community guilt over letting bad things happen. Plainfield didn't stop the Cartwright lynching. And Plainfield didn't stop little Eddie. He was not a secretive person and even joked about what he was doing. Nobody listened.

We all pay a price for this lack of attention. Every man of my generation or older has had to question his manhood. Every woman who lived through those times has considered the possibility of falling victim to such sick crimes. And everyone considers that little bit of the chopper inside of them and wonders when the next weak little Eddie will provide the next vehicle.

The Power of Doty Island

The drive from Plainfield to the Fox Valley is only about an hour long. But the cultural distance is great. The contrasts between the small sand country community and the booming industrial belt are wide and deep.

Indeed, the Fox Valley has very little North Country feel. My earlier visit to Green Bay and Oneida had put me on the edge of this burgeoning expanse of strip malls and subdivisions. Now I was in the heart of it.

It would have been easy to reject the idea that this area could be home to "northwoods" stories. But my network insisted, as they had with Green Bay, that I would find a connection. And there were many reminders of this wild past in the many activities centered on the rivers and lakes.

Despite the population growth in the Fox Valley, the area remains a center for boating, fishing, waterfowl hunting, and even sturgeon spearing. Some observers think it is also becoming the industrial and political center of Wisconsin as southeast Wisconsin's older urban centers undergo fitful transitions.

The itinerary took me to Doty island, an urbanized isle in the mouth of the upper Fox River where it empties into Lake Winnebago. Politics (and perhaps deeper forces) conspired to divide the island on a east-west axis into Menasha and Neenah parts. It was not the first time my story collection efforts brought me to Doty Island. The tale of the ancient Culdee explorers focused on the island. Many reports of haunted houses along Nicolet Street convinced me that an odd supernatural climate existed along that municipal boundary line. The lore of the first Americans also hung heavy in secret spots of the island.

Professional obligations broke up my travels after my Plainfield visit. It was a full week before other assignments took me to Appleton.

After a restful night in a hotel, I headed to meet Sherwood, a local political activist. He requested a sunrise meeting in Doty Park. When I arrived, the ducks were stirring and a light breeze brought the smell of algae and dead fish off the lake.

❦️ ❦️ ❦️

This is no ordinary ghost. Well, maybe none of them are ordinary. But it's nothing like any of the haunted house stories around here. There's a strength here. An elemental force that's way beyond the understanding of anyone in my circle. Something that is subtle in its influence and deep in its raw presence. It comes out in ways that impact every area of human life.

I know I'm going to sound paranoid here. It's going to sound like a jumble of politics, counterculture, and conspiracy stuff. Yes, I'm just a self-employed carpenter and left-libertarian gadfly in the right-wing swamp of the Fox Valley. A pre-hippie, post-beatnik, independent bohemian who's too worn-out for the New Age stuff. And yes, I did the psychedelics, the potent herbs, and all manner of chemicals. But now I go no stronger than tea.

Though I was born and raised in the area, I've always known that there was something wrong with the Fox Valley. It's just less Wisconsin than the rest of the state. Sure, we got fish fries and the Packers. But we're less progressive, less Protestant, less populist, and less libertarian. There's no place else where abortion is so reviled and the death penalty so embraced. It's like Jesuit inquisitors put something in the water.

Funny, although I'm a recovering Catholic, I learned how to piece this all together from an old Belgian priest. He showed me how it's all connected. He convinced me that the push for mines up north, the low prices for pulp, the PCBs in the water, the throwing moms off welfare, and the get-tough-on-crime stuff all flow from the same source.

I don't know if it's some old Druid thing that the Celtic Culdees brought here a thousand years ago. Or it could have been something that the Fox tribe left behind for their French enemies. I do know that some of the most powerful men in Wisconsin are connected to it.

It's *The Power*, the idea of domination, control, and subjugation. It's not empowerment, it's the ability to get others to suspend their critical faculties and to get them to ignore their self interest.

138

The priest told me that a shaman talked of a journey to the underworld to understand The Power. You need to talk to a shaman to understand that. The explanation was that a powerful fallen angel—a demon if you will—was not only cast out by the Creator, but was eradicated. But this malevolent force was so powerful that it left a residual energy capable of considerable mischief. So what you have is one incredibly ticked-off ghost of a spirit. Weird, huh?

The shaman says it was put here on the island to keep it out of harm's way. What a mistake! Who would've figured that this would become such a populated place? And who would've figured that local elites would've figured out how to tap this ghost that appears to be on crack, steroids, and PCP? A kind of evil genie in a bomb case.

Doty Island is like the old south's crossroads. It's a place where you can make deals with The Power. But he always collects in the end. Two very famous Americans came here to make deals for what they wanted. They're practically household names. I'm talking about Harry Houdini and Joe McCarthy.

Houdini came here at a very young age. An old fellow brought him. Little Harry had such a strong character that he was able to go away with a lot of energy without it poisoning his soul. He just used the energy for a very focused purpose. Even so, he had to pay the bill with his life when it came due. Everyone knows that it wasn't a pretty ending.

With Tailgunner Joe, it was really quite a different deal. There you had someone with a mean streak and a catalog of character flaws that made for an explosive mix when hooked into The Power. It built fires of hate so hot in old Joe that it just burned him up like an oil-well fire.

And through Joe, it spread that fire to others and does so to this day. There was a New Orleans businessman, a fruity type who liked to wear dresses, who Joe brought up here. That fellow was one of those shadowy figures in the assassination of President Kennedy.

Then there were the FBI officials who came. Maybe as high up as J. Edgar Hoover himself. Makes you wonder about a connection here between cross-dressing, anti-communism, and deals with The Power. Once that part of the government was involved, the secrecy lid came down. Scientists moved in and strange things started to happen.

On one hand, there was the business side. New businesses, old businesses, utilities, and research outfits—all playing partial cover for The Power. They've even found a way to generate conventional electrical power from this.

The whole Fox Valley is one big experiment for this. They have found a way to use this energy for mind control. Look at the mercury, PCBs, and other pollution around here. Look at the crazy unchecked development. Look at the bizarre politics. Anywhere else in Wisconsin this stuff alone would cause riots.

Then there's the impact on health and mental health. Check our cancer rates. Get the numbers from the women's shelters on wife-beating. Things that are public health crises elsewhere are ho-hum here.

And they're feeding The Power with souls. They've found a way to suck them right up at the point of death. They're grabbing all the fresh spirits from Fond du Lac to Green Bay.

On the other hand, there is the cult side of this, too. This is the band of rightwing nutcakes who conjure up The Power through a combination of occult practices and technology. They still gather up at Joe's grave trying to draw energy there too. But that old boy's empty. He's in The Power now.

It's reaching critical mass here. So many souls are stuffed under Doty Island that they're bursting out. That's what's happening along Nicolet Street. They're even popping up out in Lake Winnebago. This is brought to us by the same fools who build nuclear power plants without figuring out what to do with radioactive waste. Why, they're robbing tens of thousands of an afterlife on this one.

How do they get away with it? That's simple. Even with holy hell busting loose in the local spirit world, they've managed to pacify the population. After all, if you have a constituency that doesn't mind seeing grandma's house bulldozed to make way for a convenience store, what's the problem with ghosts oozing through the storm drains?

It's fair to ask how I know all these things. I use to chase ghosts like you. I know you hear lots of strange stories. The Belgian priest got me started, pointed in the right direction. He participated inside Joe McCarthy's circle. He admitted that their Cold War fanaticism allowed for an end-justifies-the-means philosophy. After all, those souls were simply soldiers in the holy war against the evils of communism. I don't know what the current rationale would be. Sort of like the military looking for a mission.

He later saw that this stuff was wrong. That it is evil to prevent a soul from uniting with its Creator. But he's still afraid to go public. He only told me because of the bond we've forged fighting the paper mills. That, and because he's dying of cancer.

So you came looking for ghosts. Tripping across the northern half of Wisconsin on a supernatural scavenger hunt. And you found some ghosts. Big whoop! You can chase your piddly little ghost stories all over the boondocks if you want. But The Power is the real story.

Mather's Shaman

My northwoods journey had granted me many brushes with the keepers of ancient perspectives on spirits. The native medicine men, lodge keepers, and pipe carriers all broadened my sense of what moved on and through the land.

My Doty Island source's urging to visit a shaman was prescient in its timing. I was to visit an area where the counties of Juneau, Jackson, and Monroe intersect. It was an area where old stories of haunting, swamp spirits, monsters, and paranormal activity were common.

Usually inquiries about such things had led me to anxious informants. Their accounts, as shown by prior narratives, run the gamut from simple historical views to complex and fantastic allegations. It was rare to have multiple sources cheerfully steer me to someone who had effectively dealt with hauntings, possessions, curses, and such. It was even rarer to run into such skills outside of tribal circles. An "exorcist" once practiced in Hillsboro and a "juju mama" once cast spells in Milwaukee. Other old Wisconsin families knew of "granny doctors," "healers," and "conjurers." But it was usually in the past tense.

The modern practitioners of these ancient arts were talked about in hushed tones. Rural people, much like their medieval European ancestors, traded embellished stories about wiccan colonies and eccentric hermits. So when a casual contact in Babcock told me to visit the Mather shaman woman, and provided testimonials, I was surprised. Others within the northwoods network vouched for her skills and devotion.

My surprise deepened when I rounded the dirt lane between two Town of Kingston cranberry bogs and saw Jessica's cottage standing on an earthen mound. The place was the exact image of my mind's

fantasy of a tidy retreat. The timber frame structure was ringed by red,
white, and jack pines, and flanked by matching clumps of white birch.
The yard was a cornucopia of herbs, vegetables, and small livestock.

Jessica stood in the doorway and was bathed in a golden light
coming from the house. A smile spilled warmth that engulfed me over
a hundred feet away. Her coppery hair wrapped her like a shawl and
provided a brilliant contrast to her white cotton dress. She, too, was
in precise conformity to my mental vision of the earthy, healing woman.

I realized that I had been coming to this place for a long time. It
was exactly what the doctor ordered.

᭞ ᭞ ᭞

Yes, I know you have many questions. You have many questions
that you do not yet know that you have. And you have places—
here and below—that you need to journey to that will fill you with
more questions.

Yes, I talk to ghosts or spirits of dead humans. I don't exorcise
them. I don't unlock their evil spells. At most, I calm them down. I look
for imbalance. It's really a health problem. The errant spirit is just a
symptom, not the disease. So when people come to me for help with
a ghost, I need to look at their whole life and environment.

I find it works to focus this work in an area I'm familiar with.
Places where I know the way of life and the energy of the land. It
wouldn't work to plunk me down in the rain forest and try to do things
the way I do them here. This swamp country is my territory. Roughly
from Necedah to Pittsville. You listen to those old independent farm
women and those bachelor woodsmen. You seek out the Ho Chunk
elders who know the secret places and the healing spirits. And then
you use the techniques that humans have used to contact spirits for
over ten thousand years. You do that through your relationship with
the earth.

That's the shaman's work. When they tell me of an old woman's
ghost crying over at Bear Bluff, I look at the treatment of women in
those families. When I hear of a lost child's spirit near Babcock, I try
to find out what's happening to the children in that neighborhood. The
same thing when I dealt with the ghost bear at Valley Junction or
the half-man, half-pig creature near Sprague.

I don't interview residents about these things. Perhaps a clarify-
ing question or two. No, my inquiries are directed at the underlying

spirits. The shaman's stock in trade is knowing how to move to that world beneath the surface of this one so as to have those conversations. Shamans journey to the world of spirits in order to meet with spirit guides. There they ask questions and receive guidance on their well-being and the welfare of others.

My most recent encounter was with a ghost of a railroad worker down at Cloverdale. An eighty-year-old man had troubled sleep and bad dreams. He asked me to help him. It turned out that the dead railroader and the retired man had worked on the Chicago Northwestern together many years ago. There was an accident and only one survivor. So there was guilt here to be dealt with in healing and a need for a spirit to communicate forgiveness.

These journeys are not hokey seances with vibrating tables. I have to send my soul to the spirit level. Therein lies the shaman's discipline.

You want to know why people are experiencing more encounters with spirits? It may not be a bad thing. Maybe people are opening up. I couldn't say why it's happening in other places. They all have their own unique energies. In this area it is mostly a matter of letting go of old hurts.

The only scary spirit problems I have been party to are from imbalances between male and female energy. The Ho Chunk grandmothers say this started when the Ojibwe came to the area. They say that after the last ice age, the Ho Chunk ancestors were squash and corn growers with balance between men and women.

The eventual dominance of meat-hunting and fur-trading was a step backwards. The densities of large animals and furbearers were not high enough to support settled communal life. The gardening of village life was pushed out by the hunt-or-die lifestyle of new tribes who moved in hunting parties or small family units.

From the spirit standpoint, the nuclear family is not a healthy, functional social unit. In the best of circumstances it is missing the wisdom and centeredness of village life. But put that unit in a run down shack in the woods, with no other supportive families nearby. Throw in some economic deprivation and, presto, you have a recipe for wife beating, child neglect, and substance abuse.

It doesn't have to end up that way. But if you're isolated you just have to work consciously to make sure it doesn't. You need the elders and the nurturing spirits. Otherwise it leaves children without social skills, ages and depresses women, and makes men paranoid and distorts their vision. That story of *The Shining* is not much of an exaggeration.

I suspect that further north you've seen how this isolation poisons life of the spirit. Often the men are going nuts and they ascribe the things they see and hear to "evil" spirits. Spirits are more gentle than that. There are no evil earth spirits. There's only the projected sociopathy and psychosis of those who can't live in harmony. That's what the unearthly spirits feed off of.

Further up north you get the men who moved there to "get away." They don't realize that what they hoped to get away from is often trapped within them. And the pieces of their souls that could help are missing. They need to be healed before the move can do any good.

So I worry more about the poisoned male spirit than about ghosts. The treaty rights battle was a good example of that. So are the petty harassments leveled at the Hmong and the hate crimes against the Amish. I wish I could reach more men or that we could find more men to become shamans. It's actually a good spirit path for a man. Once he learns the lessons, he needs no priest, no intermediary. The shaman's method empowers him to continue this spirit work on his own.

This ability is in many people. It's just been forced underground and they've lost their connection to it. It's been forced to come out in other ways. Our storytellers, our filmmakers, our playwrights, and our musicians all express that ancient yearning for the journey. When the Doors sing of breaking on through to the other side and of the riders on the storm they are hinting at the journey.

I would like to show you how to do this work. Please lie down and get comfortable. I'll darken the room and get my drum. Together, we will gather the strength to face the darkness. You'll begin that part of your journey where you'll get to talk to all the spirits who can help you. Spirits of the dead, of the animals, of the plants, and of the earth itself.

Winter Solstice Nederman

The visit to my new friend, the Mather Shaman, turned me inward. Her techniques brought me greater understanding of my journey. Perhaps more important, it also gave me greater understanding of myself. The first visit paved the way for weekly visits for several months.

Those visits slowed my hectic pace. Reflection and introspection were important medicines for a mind made feverish by the strange experiences related by sources often stranger than their tales.

A languid late summer and a reinvigorating autumn built my strength for the final phase of my investigation. Winter was about to creep up on me when I realized that I had a seasonal visit to make in Mt. Morris. A retired merchant seaman wrote to tell me that he would talk about the ghost stories in that Waushara County community. Severt insisted that his ghosts were of Nordic origin and connected to Norwegian and Danish sailors.

It seemed to be a cozy ethnic tale like the ones I had heard years before in southwest Wisconsin. The story sounded like a fitting counterpoint to my swings between ranting sources and mellow healers. As it turned out, there were community secrets, ancient connections, and contemporary conspiracies linked to Severt's tale.

He asked me to time my arrival to the day of the winter solstice. A light snow powdered the landscape as we split and stacked firewood. We caught a slight peek of sunset through the low clouds over Wautoma Swamp. We then repaired to matching recliners and brandy snifters in front of a crackling fire.

🔥 🔥 🔥

You've heard a few stories, haven't you? Maybe getting just a bit jaded? Run into assorted nuts, fruits, cranks, and kooks, right?

I'm not going to swear on a bible that all of the stuff I'm about to tell you is real. Heck, I don't know. I'm just telling you what I've heard and seen. Thirty-two years at sea—listening to watch mates in fog and to galley scuttlebutt—and you get to know that everybody has their own way of looking at things.

We've an odd hidden history here. Our Norwegian families and our few Danes were mostly farmers. But there is a tradition linked to the sea. That's because it was a way of life that illegitimate sons could make their way in. It was a place where an orphaned young man could get food and shelter.

It was sons of Mt. Morris that helped start the Lake Seamen's Union. It was sons of Mt. Morris who helped spread the work of the *Forkyndelse* or the sailors missionary society. Perhaps because of their travels, or perhaps because the old stories served as their family connection, they kept the old lore alive when no other Norwegians in this area remembered the slightest shred of their heritage beyond lutefisk.

There were Larsens and Hansons who worked whalers. Johnsons on the last of the clippers around the Horn. Petersons with Dewey at Manila Bay. The boys were never acknowledged by their fathers, and in some cases never knew who they were. But they faithfully celebrated Syttende Mai and visited the Sons of Norway lodges whenever they could.

They told stories about Aegir, god of the north seas and his daughters, the gray waves, who take sailors to the bottom to seduce them. They talked about the supernatural creatures: *hulders, nissers, fossegrimers*, and *nokkers*. They whispered about the curses of the heks, or witch. They prayed to be delivered from the hands of *gamle-erik*, the devil.

But the story that bound those boys to the Mt. Morris area was that of the solstice ghosts. These were always talked about as two distinct personalities: the Oberman and the Nederman. The Oberman is the ghost of the summer solstice. He is the ghost of positive energy, of long sunny days, and of the warmth that greens the land. This ghost is friendly and helpful. He is sometimes called "the happy farmer."

The Nederman is the ghost of the winter solstice. He is the ghost of the dark, of short days, when depressed moods come from confinement indoors. The psychologists call this seasonal affected disorder. But here we call him "the night walker." He takes souls away.

Seaman get to know that such ghosts appear at many places throughout the northern hemisphere. You have spirits of the longest day and shortest day among the Siberians, Lapps, and Aleuts. Among some of the Great Lakes tribes you have the spirits of the strawberry moon and of sleeping bear moon.

It could be our two local ghosts have this old Indian connection. Otherwise, I don't know why these things would go back so far in Mt. Morris history. You still hear of Indians coming into the area and conducting ceremonies. There was a story from the turn of the century. They say an old Winnebago medicine man came back from Nebraska and went out to the hill that later became the ski run. I guess he stayed out there singing and drumming for days in the snow. Then he started howling. Finally, they took him away in a straitjacket.

After that, there was even more talk of the Nederman working during the winter solstice. It seems like that was the time when the old people passed away and when the diseases took the livestock. Then we had people making runes on stones. It was more than writing, it was magic. We had several old women take up the old Norwegian ratwife tradition. That's the old crones' work of healing plants, charming animals through music and song, and spells.

It's funny, they say the ordinary ghosts are more active at summer solstice. Some even talked about the Oberman throwing a party for all the local ghosts on the eve of the longest day. At winter solstice only the Nederman is active.

We even developed our own traditions about communicating with the spirit world on summer solstice eve. You could stop an annoying ghost by standing at the church at midnight on that day and reading from the Bible. It was also the night to talk to your dead relatives if you had a charm from a ratwife. But you had to promise not to reveal the conversation to anyone. The night was called Jonsok after John the Baptist. Shades of Davey Jones!

You can think of the Oberman of the summer solstice as a quaint little ritual for a bunch of farmers. Something of a bygone day. Ah, but the Nederman, there you have something that's still in the air, as it were. Like most rural areas, we have a variety of outsiders who've adopted our little community. It's surprising how quickly they pick up on our old traditions and splice on their own little features.

The local oldtimers and the clergy call them a cult. By Neptune's beard, I'd call them more an overeducated little clique of wine-imbibing wife swappers with vivid imaginations. They got their ghosts mixed up with the UFO's, comets, chariots of fire, and end-of-the-world stuff. They even think that the sailing traditions evident in these stories are references to space travel!

They see the Nederman as a spaceship pilot. They think that his visits are meant to gather passengers for distant destinations. But they see the human body as a impediment to space travel. As they say, the soul doesn't need a spacesuit. I don't know why we dumb sailors never thought about that. Why bother with lifeboats?

I visited one meeting with this group. Well, it was part meeting, part church service, and part psychic fair. They had a reading of the minutes, a channeling of the Nederman's voice through a ninety-pound woman, and some singing.

Their songs were all adaptations of old hymns and modern popular songs. Sailors have done the same thing for years, only with dirty and rebellious lyrics. They did something pretty bizarre with "Jesus Loves Me." But their rendition of the red robin song was pretty catchy

147

and tied into a comet they were waiting for. It went something like, "when the Hale-Bopp comet comes bop, bop, bopping along, along . . . they'll be no more dying when our old worn bodies are gone, are gone," and so on.

So how do you judge this stuff? Do the things we think of as spirits originate in space? Is what we think of as a near-death experience a form of space travel? Are angels high-tech travel guides?

I can't answer any of these questions. I can just tell you that I've seen the Nederman do a low-level fly-by over Willow Creek. I know that my new neighbors seem goofy. But underneath the layers of crap there's the core of older stuff I told you about. I mean to tell you, no old salt lets the bilge of missionaries or church affect our connection to God. I know I'll see the Nederman at the end.

Butte des Morts Skeletons

Battlefield ghosts are present at a number of Wisconsin sites. Part of the legend of Strawberry Island at Lac du Flambeau relates to such ghosts. Stories in southwest Wisconsin from Black Hawk War days place battlefield ghosts at Spafford Creek, Bloody Run, Wisconsin Heights, and Bad Axe. Some would even say that the hauntings at Porte des Morts and Prairie du Chien are battlefield ghosts. Battlefield ghost stories range from prehistoric feuds with Vikings to intertribal conflict to the fur trade skirmishes involving the British and French to the American occupation of Wisconsin.

Little is known about the early intertribal battles. American Indian storytellers will only rarely speak of the tribes pushed out, or wiped out, by other tribes. In some stories, the wiped-out tribes are reduced to nameless bands of drifting spirits destined to roam their old territories forever.

It is not common for European Americans to take up the stories of these intertribal warrior ghosts unless there is a sufficient body of local lore to serve as a bridge for adaptation. It is even rarer for a

European American family to serve as a custodian for traditions lost to their original keepers.

Again I was faced with the anomaly of an essentially rural, outdoor tale on the periphery of the urbanized Fox Valley. Unlike the haunted warehouses of nearby Oshkosh or the rail ghosts on tracks taken over by the Wisconsin Central, there were ancient themes connected to the original inhabitants. All the signs pointed to another out-of-place northwoods story.

The patio doors of Chester's recreation room faced a wind-whipped Lake Butte des Morts. A few foolish geese circled in a slushy inlet. He poured two stiff drinks of bourbon. He had a haunted look, down to the dark circles under his eyes and a furrowed brow. Here was a self-admitted simple man with a complicated and prophetic tale.

🔥 🔥 🔥

This isn't like one of the deals where a mysterious Indian medicine man drops by to scare the white folks with news of an old curse. Most of those medicine men are named Vinny and have ancestors in Sicily. This is a family tradition that goes back to pioneer times. Supposedly great-great-grandmother Esther cared for a dying Indian woman. The Indian woman was called Bone Woman. Esther wrote all about Bone Woman in a diary that I've got here.

I'd be the first to admit that I don't know diddly about ghosts, demons, spirits, and such, or what separates one from the other. I use to think all that stuff was a bunch of hoo-ha. Good for campfire stories and that's about it. But I feel different now.

Finding the old lady's diary was part of it. But, more important, I was also influenced by events in the last year. Stuff I've experienced and stuff others have told me. I'm sure something weird is going on. I'm just not prepared to say what it really means.

I guess you have to go back to the beginning. You know, back to the big battle involving the Indians. Mound of the Dead and all that. Supposedly so many were killed that they were stacked in a big pile. But there are some things about old Esther's diary that make it sound like she thought that the place was more like an Aztec pyramid where people were brought to be killed.

This Bone Woman—Winnebago or Menominee survivor or whatever—talked about the bone people. I took that to mean animated skeletons. Esther's diary suggests pretty much the same thing. The diary talks about Bone Woman's gift for prophecy. She predicted that Butte des Morts would become a collection place for skeletons. They would actually come here from other places. They're supposed to start skeleton warrior dances and sing and drum.

The signs in this prophecy say those things will start to happen when the wolves run in the streets of the white man's town and the owls hoot within his cities. Those things, as you know, are starting to pass.

There's a prophecy within the prophecy. The dead from the so-called battle were described in terms of willing victims of ritual combat. Supposedly they knew the day of white dominance was coming. The casualties were to serve as the nucleus of a skeleton army to prepare for another change. All that was foretold by a bright planet— probably Mars—that served as the basis for a holy man's vision. They knew back then that the white man would sweep the old world away. But they didn't fear it, it was just part of nature's cycle.

But now we're close to the next part of the cycle. The skeletons are getting restless. No, I'm not making this up. It's happening in lots of different ways. It seems like bones are starting to pop up all over. Every time somebody digs a foundation or tears down an old building there are bones found. They're turning up in places where it is unlikely they were buried. So how did they get there? That's a damn good question.

I think they're moving. You heard me. Moving through and in the ground. Changing from one species of skeleton to another. Coming apart in one place and assembling themselves in another.

I've got neighbors with dreams, visions, and other subconscious references to skeletons. Old farmers tell me they see skull shapes in the clouds. Fishermen out on Lake Butte des Morts talk about whole schools of swimming skeletons. One neighbor lady told me about a strange dream she had. In it, a whole mob of skeletons was running down Brooks Road. It was almost like an organized marathon.

My son had a nightmare of skeletons tunneling through the earth. He said some were raising bumps like moles. Others were moving through solid rock. A few had soft bones and wiggled their way through dirt like worms. In the nightmare they were coming from all directions.

As for me, I thought I saw a bunch while walking the dog in the woods out on Plummer Point. I know you'll think I'm crazy, but I thought I saw some carrying on like it was a skeleton mardi gras. Dancing, jumping, and goosing each other in the butt. Well, in the pelvic bones. Kind of jug music coming out their mouths and playing each

150

other's bones like drums and xylophones. I just about lost bladder control and the dog ran home. Then, zip, zip, they're gone with no evidence they were ever there.

It's not like we never had any ghost stories around here. There's supposed to be a hanging ghost in Winnecone. I've heard of a drowning phantom under the bridges in Oshkosh. And there's supposed to be a haunting up on Green Meadow Road that drives women insane. But nothing like hordes of skeletons up the wazoo!

Who knows what this means? And what can we do if it's like it says in Esther's diary and it all means the end of the world? She wrote about that as if it wasn't entirely a bad thing. As if it happened a number of times before and will happen countless times again. Almost as if she saw it as renewal.

Let me read the Bone Woman's final prophecy as Esther recorded it:

"When the old ways are gone and even the children of the Indians shall have forgotten the names and language of their fathers, then a time will come when the white man will be a swarm of locusts on the land. When the white man has fouled the air, water, and earth, the bones of Indians shall come back to life. The spirits in the bones of all the past generations will come among the white man and haunt him. The bone spirits shall come to dwell in the white man's children. Heed this warning! Honor the bone spirits. The dead have power over the living!"

I suppose we'll just have to wait and see if this amounts to anything. On the other hand, if you have a home remedy to get rid of the buggers, I'm all ears.

PART V

Portage to the South

Ho Chunk Tricksters

Spring brought wild asparagus to the country roadsides before I again resumed my quest. The intervening winter was devoted to weekly trips to visit Jessica and have her use the shaman's techniques to journey to the lower world. Almost every spirit I had encountered on my expeditions inhabited some niche of the shaman's other worlds and could be contacted in those realms.

There was the conceit that I was getting closer to answering my many questions and discerning my unified theory of all northwoods supernatural occurrences. Why was there this pervasive belief in the marshalling of ghosts—from Lac Vieux Desert to Butte des Morts— and why was it connected to the fear of environmental contamination and political conspiracy?

Just like the physicists closing in on a unified theory which explains the universe, I felt I was close to understanding. In fact, I sensed that the physicists' answer was, in large part, my answer. Yet our human minds did not seem large enough to grasp the subtleties of time, space, and matter that held the answer.

Instinct repeatedly pointed toward the influence of location, be it physical properties or the resonance of unseen forces. Along with that was the recurrent linkage to the land's original inhabitants. If there were ancient clues about this process, was it not logical to ask the descendants of the first people?

My sources pushed me to Farrell, a Ho Chunk businessman in Juneau County. He asked me to meet him on a slow Saturday morning at an outdoorsmen's bar called the Star Route Lounge on Highway 21, just west of Necedah. Despite the early hour, he expected me to keep pace with him on alligator kebobs. He agitated himself with coffee while I held his energy at bay with Old Style.

☙ ☙ ☙

Ho Chunk are what's left of the original people of Wisconsin. We're what's left of the life at the end of the ice age. We're the grandchildren of the cave painters and mound builders. All the other tribes wandered or were pushed here later.

155

We have the oldest Wisconsin stories and the oldest Wisconsin secrets. We tended the ancient spirits and watched the passing of the large beasts. We even shaped the landscape in the southern two-thirds of what is now Wisconsin. Not just by the building of mounds, although there's plenty of significance in that. And hidden meaning too. But also through our raised-bed gardens, our burning of prairies, and our hunting methods.

This includes what we call the bear groves, cleared areas under and around massive oak trees. Mostly white oaks. But any kind of oak with acorns that would bring the bears to feed. So we made these as bait spots, but it helped create the oak savannas.

This has a connection to the Bear Clan and the trickster. It was the Bear Clan that maintained these clearings and supervised the bear hunts. They were operating on the trickster's instructions. That gave rise to the clan's police function that continues to this day.

This trickster was called Wak Dejunk Agah. He was the first shaman after the ice age. He was more in the tradition of Merlin and the European wizards than the tradition of tribal medicine men. I say that because he used magic in ways that were political.

He was at the core of organizing the mound-builders' culture. Some say he directed their construction. Some say he used them for magic, astronomy, astrology, and human sacrifice. Yes, you heard me right. Human sacrifice. That's why there's a Wisconsin connection to the Aztecs and Mayans. The mounds are related to the pyramids. And the inspiration for both came from the same place: the wizard's other world.

It's a story of good intentions gone bad. The trickster's magic was, at first, a good thing. But somewhere in there the power of the magic became a drug. That's when he went from the healing side to the dark side. That's what all dictators and mass murderers are about. It always comes down to the dark side of power.

The era of the mound-builders ended when the Bear Clan revolted and killed the trickster. They lured him into the marsh country west of here and trapped him in a flooded pit. They must have had some powerful magic in order to do that.

But maybe not powerful enough. The trickster was no sooner dead in human form then he popped up in spirit form. He's been a plague on the Ho Chunk and all those close to us ever since. He threw us into war against many people. He caused the legendary battle

156

with Red Horn, who was probably a Viking raider. When the English and French came later, he weakened our medicine and opened us up to their epidemics.

We shrank as a tribe and became vulnerable to foolishness. Our unity disappeared and we developed factions and infighting. We flip-flopped between the French, British, and, later, the Americans. We even got entangled on both sides of the Black Hawk War. Some Sac think the Ho Chunk egged on Black Hawk's adventure to set him up for the slaughter. Lot of hard feelings there.

The trickster continued to do his work on us. He helped manipulate the removals to the west. He set up the loss of many of our cranberry bogs to white businessmen. He poisoned people with fights over tribal politics and casino money.

There is a way to fight back. A way to get our medicine back. It's a spiritual path. It's the path of peyote. It is a sacred path for us that goes back thousands of years among native people. It's a path of visions and renewal. It clears the mind and lets you get close to the spirits.

Ordinarily, the spirits are helpful. And if you do encounter a bad one you have other spirits to call on to get you out of a jam. That's what happened to me.

Do you know how peyote ritual works? First off, a roadman is in charge. He runs the all-night ceremony. It runs ten to twelve hours. It's a lot of sitting in the tepee. A prayer is sung. The peyote medicine is passed around. Then another singing prayer. More peyote is passed around. And so on. This goes on all night until a woman brings water in the morning. Then people go out in the fresh morning air to cool off. Then they come back in for a meal.

When I finally learned to journey with peyote it was an amazing thing. I saw a shining city in a dark abyss. It was as if I was flying toward that place. I was drawn there and I felt out of control. When I got closer, I saw the place was covered in bones, skulls, and snakes. They were all shining and glistening.

There was an odd-looking man on a high tower. He looked as if he had only one good eye and an empty socket. He wanted me to come inside. But fortunately, a bear showed up in my vision and growled loudly. The bear spoke Ho Chunk and told me that the old man was the trickster.

The bear showed me the other faces of the trickster. How the trickster masquerades as other spirits. How he even gets inside the white

157

man's ghosts. How he draws power from a certain territory. It's an upside down triangle when you plot it on a map of Wisconsin. Draw a line from Green Bay to Neillsville, Then connect those two points to Portage.

I don't know if it's everywhere in that area. What I've learned about so far is connected to specific hidden marsh sites. Mostly in the Necedah area that I know best. But I also figured out where the shining city is. It's Columbia prison down at Portage!

But come to think of it, the triangle is loaded with prisons. One practically at each corner, Columbia at Portage, one at Green Bay, and Jackson at Black River Falls. Not to mention nearby ones at Oshkosh, Oxford, and Waupun not far away. Are you finding anything near those places? Any clues about odd stuff in those prisons?

See, I just don't know enough about those spots outside of my area. I can only tell you how it works here with the trickster. With the local ghosts and the mysteries. Somebody needs to look at all this stuff and put it together.

First, there's the stuff about collecting souls. There's a Fox River soul carrier, a Horicon Marsh grim reaper, and Castle Rock wolf pack that all seem to perform that role. Have you ever heard anything as weird as that?

Then there's the trickster's takeover of the older ghosts. I don't mean just the Ho Chunk ones. In fact, it seems he's done more to control the ghosts of your people. There's a Lemonweir River wraith, a Juneau County ditch goblin, the Petenwell Dam floater or drowned body phantom, and the burnt-up pioneer family at Buckhorn State Park. That's just for starters. The trickster is manipulating those and more. Seen anything like that before?

With the mysteries, who knows what's really going on there? It's prime territory around here for that. Where can you find as many lonely, fern-lined dirt lanes through jack pine and aspen? This was the bed of old glacial Lake Wisconsin after the big melt. This was the prime nesting area for the passenger pigeon. It is still the habitat of unique populations of osprey and sharp-tailed grouse.

There are hundreds of abandoned farms in this territory. Many were seized for taxes during the Great Depression. Many farmers were warped and made bitter by the hard work and poverty brought by this infertile land.

Strange things happened on those back lanes. People went missing. There's always been the talk of the murders, the tortures, the drownings, and the disappearances. Especially from here down to the Dells and Portage.

During peyote journeys, I found the trickster behind many things. He's somehow connected to the expansion of the bombing range at Fort McCoy. There are incidents there and at Camp Douglas—which the government covers up—that have a link to this supernatural force. We have people from times in the past popping up through his interference. He's a factor in those incidents where snowmobilers go through the ice on the Wisconsin River and don't pop up again until spring thaw. And we have his ongoing role in destabilizing the Ho Chunk nation.

But I've also come to see he is focused on Wisconsin Dells and Portage. It's like he draws some energy from those locations. With the Dells, it's almost like the garish nature of the place pleases him. With Portage, it's something else. Maybe something in the prison. Maybe something that happened because the old canal connected the water of the Great Lakes with the waters of the Mississippi. Something about mingling elements that will make the area unlivable. I'll have to use the peyote journey to clear those things up.

The trickster's power doesn't extend south of Portage. It's like he's banned from the old prairie country of the mounds and the caves to the south. But it's also as if he keeps the good spirits of that area out of the pine woods and marshes of the north. If things were in balance, there would be a flow of spirits both ways. When my people first lived in this land of Wisconsin, there was only a transition in the landscape, not the line you find drawn between ways of life, economics, and politics today.

There's a battle coming. I've seen that through the peyote. If we can't get the good people on both sides of the line to work together, both places will become unlivable.

Go down to the Dells, go to Portage, and figure out what's going one. Find out how we get across that line. Before you go, spend the night and make a journey with me. Take the medicine and learn to recognize the faces of Wak Dejunk Agah.

159

Sleepers

Nausea and lightheadedness plagued my morning drive from Necedah to Germania. A brief stop at a Westfield cafe for coffee and aspirin partially cleared the mental fog. The ritual medicine journey brought me only a vision of an antiseptic empty room—that and a headache.

The next stop was as yet undetermined. There were reports of ghosts in the eastern end of Marquette County. A few sites were mentioned. A source for more information was named. But it was all left very vague. The Westfield stop served as an information gathering opportunity. It grew quiet along the cafe counter when I asked questions about ghosts. When I followed up with inquiries about my potential source, a few epithets were flung my way.

It turned out my next informant was not a popular fellow. He had been a local lawyer. He had dipped into a few estate trusts and had entangled himself in a few real estate development schemes. He had made numerous enemies and had lost his law license.

A nervous waitress made a passing comment that held out hope of assistance. When the breakfast crowd thinned out she took a cigarette break on the stool next to mine. Her hushed tone suggested multiple layers of concern for customer sensibilities. A dissenting view, a little-known family tie, or an illicit relationship? Her tugging at her skirt gave a hint at the latter explanation.

She told of a distinguished gentleman and admitted an acquaintance. Her quick blush confirmed my guess about her connection to the object of my search. She poured forth an unsolicited testimonial defense of her friend and insisted that he was the target of persecution. When she learned the nature of my inquiry she pronounced her friend as an expert in such matters and hastened to give me directions as growls at the counter sent her scurrying to refill coffee mugs.

The enormous motor home was parked on an unmarked lane on the Germania side of Comstock Lake, just as the waitress told me a half-hour earlier in Westfield. The poorly maintained rich man's toys spoke volumes about falls from affluence and grace. Anthony looked up from the undersized fish that he was cleaning only long enough to determine that I was not the local conservation warden.

He looked up briefly when I revealed the purpose of my visit. He brightened when I mentioned the Westfield waitress. He beamed when I flattered his expertise. He chortled heavily when I expressed surprise about the local hostility toward him.

◖ ◖ ◖

You never make anyone happy when you are a country criminal defense lawyer. Half the people are angry at you for getting acquittals for defendants they dislike. The other half hate you because you failed to save the local football coach from the eighty-year sentence. Never mind that the D.A. had videotape of the coach under the bleachers with each one of the cheerleaders.

Well, I must confess I am not overly fond of the local half-wits. They seldom paid their fees after I had their drunk driving charges dismissed. So to eat, I was constantly having to draft wills for old ladies who left fortunes to cats.

Excuse me, I digress. I know that you are interested in the eerie side of my former professional life. You would not think that a lawyer would have occasion to delve into ghost matters.

You would be wrong in my case. I came back from flying P-38s in the South Pacific in World War Two, whipped through law school, and set up a practice. Thought I would be a judge or maybe even a congressman someday. Instead, I had to hustle to pay off all the ex-wives. I had ghosts in my cases right from the start.

The first one was a bachelor farmer who killed his mother. He said his grandmother's ghost told him to do it. Prison was the best option for him. He would have been lynched by his uncles and cousins.

After that I had wife-beaters coached by ghosts. Drunks who let spirits—no pun intended—drive their cars. Child molesters, cattle thieves, and moonshiners. Even a fellow who said he wasn't really robbing the tavern, he was simply helping a ghost recover an inheritance.

At first I thought they were just nuts. But as the years went by I had more opportunity to use psychiatric experts. In the mid-1950s, I had two clients who torched their houses and barns, claiming some threatening hauntings. The shrink told me they did not have the usual delusional symptoms. He said they were quite normal farmers who believed what they said.

More of these types came my way over the years. Maybe one or two a year. Other lawyers started to send me the clients with problems

161

of this kind. The lawyers thought these clients were all kooks and that I was a head case myself from the war.

Some patterns started to emerge. Almost all my haunted clients seemed first to experience contact with ghosts while they were dreaming. Yes, while they were sleeping soundly in their own beds. These spirits would come repeatedly in dreams. Then they would come as a presence into the bedrooms and wake these people up. That is usually when the real trouble began.

These nocturnal bedroom spirits were so common in parts of Marquette, Green Lake, and Waushara counties that the old boys had a name for them. They called them sleepers. Sometimes because they just crawled into bed with people and caught forty winks themselves.

Now a lot of these sleepers came in female form. Mostly attractive young women. So it was natural that I first thought that these ghosts served the same function for bachelor farmers as a copy of a girlie magazine in the outhouse. To stiffen their resolve as it were.

But it was more complicated than that. And a lot more problematic from a legal standpoint. These sleepers—if you believe they exist—seem to egg on a lot of seamy and disgusting crimes. Stuff that you do not even want to admit could ever happen. If you have been to Plainfield, you do not need me to paint a picture for you.

The lawyer's dilemma, as you know, is what to do with knowledge of crimes committed by a client. The emotional ranting, the rambling casual conversations, and the law office confessions all fell within what I regard as privileged attorney-client communications which I am not at liberty to discuss.

But I can tell you about the kinds of things I heard. Among the common threads of the worst offenders—the ones with the sickest crimes—is their belief that they have had ghost lovers. Visitors between the sheets who had more tricks than a Manila madam.

Now this is not a bolt out of the blue. These experiences go back to ancient times. Some might say back to the serpent in the garden. In classical times there was the incubus, a male spirit who lies with sleeping women and impregnates them. The offspring are often evil and possessed of supernatural abilities. It was said that sorcerers sometimes resulted from such unions.

While I still hear of these male spirits sleeping with human females, this is somewhat less common today. I find the roles reversed these days. It is men who host nocturnal visitors in my dirty little world. And it is men who seem to be twisted by the experience.

The ancient legends ascribed this destruction of the male character to one Lilith, Adam's soulless first wife. She gave birth only to demons and soon left Adam and joined forces with Satan. She was blamed for restless sleep. Some even thought she collected semen.

Today there are figurative, if not literal, daughters of Lilith who carry on this work. They are the succubi, sexually hungry female spirits who seem to include ghosts of mortals and beings more demonic in nature. I have known men who complain about having to satisfy whole groups of such creatures.

These female sleepers are a recurrent theme in crimes within my knowledge in Berlin, Green Lake, Montello, Omro, and Princeton. There is something in these things connected to the strangest of male urges. Everything from the sadistic torturers to the Peeping Toms.

It is a sleazy business dealing with sex offenders. Especially the rapists and child molesters. Even though I have no qualms about stiffing the IRS or giving a gift to a judge, I am not fond of the perverts. I have my standards and thought many a time that the worst of sex offenders might as well be shot.

These crimes are crimes of power, not sex. They are the ultimate method of stealing a person's spirit. Often that spirit is never restored. One must wonder where that spirit goes.

These are strange crimes. They are both under-reported and over-reported. I have known women who have been assaulted three, four, five or more times in their lives without so much as a police report. It often starts with an uncle or older cousin, then a date-raping boyfriend, and finally ends up with a co-worker or boss. You would be surprised how common a story this is among attractive women. I can sometimes detect a fragile and remote quality to such victims.

Then there is the other side of the coin. The false reports of such crimes. The falsely accused are violated, too. Their lives are often ruined, their reputations destroyed, and their families ostracized within the communities. Their accusers have the usual low motives for lying: revenge, hysteria, attention-seeking, covering up other illicit relationships, and the deflection of paternity issues during pregnancy. One such accuser later admitted to me that the late night visits of a sleeper drover her to make the accusation.

I realize this all sounds very, very odd. But I have two more items to recount which shake me to my foundations. They stem from a case that I first became involved in some ten years ago. A rather macabre case that I need not outline. The perpetrator was my client.

Before trial he hold me a fantastic story about ghost orgies out on the fringe of Germania Marsh. He said he started with the sleepers at home and gradually was able to join them out in the marsh. He painted a hellish picture of ghouls subjecting the bodies of dead victims and the subconscious of live victims to unspeakable acts. He said his crimes were the mechanism to provide fresh souls to these lustfests.

Eventually my client was sentenced to Colombia down at Portage. I visited him there a few times. No, I am not a hand-holder. It was a good way to build your reputation and pull in referrals. On my last visit there, he told me he would send me a sleeper. And that he would see me out at the marsh. He died a month after that.

I did not think much about it for a long time. I have had disgruntled clients threaten me more directly than that. When I had the first dream with a sleeper it came as a profound shock. I thought myself immune from the brain dysfunction, biochemical imbalance, and psychological vulnerability of the dull-witted who fill the prisons. And I flatter myself that, at my age I have no unfulfilled needs that would prompt such dreams.

At first I thought it was simply a matter of hearing about such things for years. But in my situation it was different. My sleeper came in the form of a lost love of my youth, a young woman who died in a car wreck while I was in the South Pacific. There was nothing foul or ominous abut it. No, it was thoroughly tender and sweet. Goodness, my current lady friend would faint away if she knew about this.

She would be even more shocked to find out that I am to father a child with that lost love in my dreams. Does this put me one step closer to that gang in the marsh? What exactly will I be fathering?

Reflections of the White Buffalo

Mirrors and looking glasses occupy an ancient role in consideration of the supernatural. Early mirrors played a part in occult practice. Many demonic and ghostly forces reportedly could not be seen in mirrors. Other spiritual entities could be glimpsed only by virtue of their reflections.

Reflected and refracted light are as much a part of ghost lore as shadow and mist. While castle mirrors are in short supply in Wisconsin, bounced and distorted images on bodies of water pop up in many ghost stories in rural areas. Lakes, rivers, ponds, potholes, and puddles find a place in our sightings of strange things. Even fetid pools viewed downward through outhouse holes launch horrid visions into little-told stories.

Reports of reflections along the Wisconsin River near Wisconsin Dells suggested a variety and frequency beyond that of the musty tales handed down by great-grandparents. The stories went further than the usual conventions of drowned lovers and pioneer boatmen in rippling portrait on the waters.

Intrigued as I was by the promise of new variations on old themes, I was somewhat reluctant to include Wisconsin Dells on my itinerary. The distance from Germania to the Dells could not be measured in miles alone. A more fundamental question demanded an answer: did a story set in the Dells merit inclusion in a collection of northwoods tales?

Even the cities I had visited to sniff out the prior stories stood in some sort of relationship to the northwoods. Be they papermill towns, wood product manufacturing centers, or aspiring industrial parks, they were part of a historic northland and their stories rested on those connections. In the Dells, I encountered the echoes of the driftless ridge country to the southwest and the prairie hum of the farmland to the southeast. Was it a place apart from those regions and the northwoods, or a blend of all those things?

A week passed after my Germania visit before I found time to search out the Dells story. The drive up Highway 12 did not put me in a northwoods mood. The tidy hill-nestled farms of central Sauk County were followed by the visual assault of Lake Delton's "attractions." When I arrived at Steamboat Rock my head was swimming.

Dale, a large and jolly member of the Ho Chunk Nation, helped soothe my feverish brain. As we watched the river ripples, he put me at ease with jokes and his interesting personal history. A veteran of the navy's "brown water fleet" in Vietnam's Mekong Delta, he grew up on the water and remained close to it. In between stints on Mississippi tugs and the amphibious "Wisconsin Ducks" tour boats, he dealt blackjack at the casino, worked in the Winnebago museum, tended bar in the tourist traps, and drove a school bus.

We waited for the "green flash," a peculiar distortion of light just before sunset. This is a common feature in paranormal sightings near *water. It is present in stories at Lone Rock, Wyalusing, Ellison Bay, and Port Wing. While we waited, Dale filled me in on the place of the Dells within the northwoods scheme of things.*

🌿 🌿 🌿

They call me Dale of the Dells. As in my Norwegian neighbor's version of "hells bells, it's Dale of the Dells." He's the one who first told me of these reflections in the water along here. He knows all the ghost stories around here.

The local Norwegians stand in a good relation to the Ho Chunk. They once ran off the government to protect their Ho Chunk neighbors. Not like those old New Englanders who liked to convert Indians—to Christians, to good citizens, to factory workers or whatever. Not like the first Germans, who liked to wipe us out, then mourn us and romanticize us. And not like the Irish, who liked to get drunk and stupid with us, then fight us. What I like about the Norwegians is that they're just not ambitious enough for the foolishness of the other groups.

Those Norskies figure into a lot of our stories. There are a few that wouldn't have been preserved without them. There are spirit stories at Rocky Arbor, Elephant Rock, and Corning Lake that they are tangled up in.

They were ahead of us on these reflections. Old Bill started to tell me about them ten years ago. He told me he saw an old-time Indian war party reflected in the water. War clubs, painted faces, and deerskin jockstraps. Of course when he looked over to the other bank, he saw no sign of a physical source for this reflection.

My first thought was: too much brandy for Bill. But then I heard another report of a ghostly reflection. A cousin of mine confided that he saw a medicine man doing a pipe ceremony reflected in the waters beyond Stand Rock. Then I heard little snippets of stories about reflected ghosts of trappers and traders. I didn't discount them, but I still wasn't convinced that it was anything more than temporary light patterns. Sort of like when the clouds blow together to look like Barbara Bush for five minutes.

Of course my attitude changed when I saw reflected ghosts myself. Right across the way here. Around this time of day. It was a group of black robes, old French priests, walking along in a line. I even thought I heard a Latin chant!

Well, that was the first of many times that I saw reflections. And you know what? It was never exactly the same thing twice. I saw some things that I still don't know how to describe. Saw some things that keep me up nights.

These reflections, I believe, are a series of prophecies. Kind of a Nostradamus writing on water. That's what I figured out after I first saw the reflection of the white buffalo. I saw that and the next thing you know I heard of one born in Wisconsin. That made a believer out of me.

Most of these prophecies are warnings to think about the consequences of our actions. To think about the future generations. To be gentle and respectful of each other. To create a vision of a healthy world and work on that vision.

That's why it's not crazy to be seeing things. When someone from the mainstream says a person is seeing things, they mean he is crazy, don't they? But I'm here to tell you that we should pray every day that more people start seeing things. I've come to realize that it's not seeing things that is the problem. If we can't see the spirits warning us, begging us, and even taking horrible form to scare us, then we're hopelessly disconnected from ourselves and the things around us.

Each time I see a reflection of the white buffalo in another scene, I see another warning about despoiling the land. Or a caution about the false gods of progress and the whoredom of development. Or about the spiritual toll people pay when this disconnection plays out in our communities. Where do you think the crime and the insanity comes from? Our places become soulless and so do we!

That's why these reflections are happening at the Dells. The Dells stands as the false north. It's a trick pulled on tourists. And you could almost laugh at that. But the trick is on us, too, because it's also a warning about what could happen all through the north country. Any place where some fast talkers can stir up a frenzy about lakeshore property value and tourist dollars, well, there you could go right down this road.

And if you want my buffalo nickel's work, that's a bigger danger than mines, or papermills, or government boondoggles. Yes, you heard me, it's worse than mining! Maybe worse than a radioactive waste dump!

A mine is a horrible gash in the earth. But it has limits. And we can get people to fight it. Even failing in that fight creates powerful visual medicine against the next mine. But what happens when a gas station is joined by a fast-food place, then a motel, and then a miniature golf course? It's a sneaky little process and hardly anybody notices. The next thing you know, there are miles of it.

Even the oldest Dells ghost story is jumbled up in our out-of-control development problem. Have you heard about the Devil's Hitching Post? It's not far from here. The place is called Elephants Rock now. There was a conscious name change done to please the sensitive tourists of the late 1800s.

The old Devil's Hitching Post had a few too many scary traditions connected to it. The earlier Ho Chunk trickster spirits. The drunken French traders who killed each other there. The English soldiers who were murdered in their sleep by the Kickapoo renegades. The Norwegian homesteaders who disappeared here. All ghosts of the place.

The Norwegians had a belief that if you tethered a horse there, then the angel of death would come for your soul. Apparently there was at least one settler killed there by a mysterious black horse.

That should have told visitors something, but it didn't. Instead, people kept coming and using and taking. They first robbed the watery canyons of silence with the engines of their boats. Then they shattered the solitude with the construction of hotels. Finally, they built so many distractions and signs that the beauty of the place was buried beneath the crap. It became possible to visit the place and remain totally unaware of its special character.

The lesson for me is that the Dells was a special spirit place. It was a place that was to be visited reverently. It was not meant to be a place to live it up or to junk up.

When we see the reflections of the white buffalo on the river it could be telling us many things. It could be telling us it is leading the spirits out of this dead-spirit place that man has built. Or it could be telling us that the spirits are about to rise up in revolt at our injury to this place.

But for me, the reflection of the white buffalo is a personal sign. I know it is calling me to a different life. It is a sign that I am not to be a part of anything else that spoils this sacred place.

Columbia'a Imprisoned Spirits

The prior story set in Wisconsin Dells could easily have been the last chapter of this book. Such an ending might have left me with more unanswered questions, but it might have been tidier and less disturbing.

Despite some clues and some prodding from sources, I was as reluctant to place Portage with a northwoods collection as I had been with the Dells. In spite of the years of driving past the sign on Highway 51 designating Portage as the place "where the north begins," I was not a believer. Time spent in that town as a state employee and a railroad worker did little to convince me that it had any north-country flavor.

It turned out that the equation was reversed in my mind and on the roadside sign. It is not the place where the north begins. It is the place where the north ends. You must look closely for signs of the north-woods around Portage. But south of the city there is a clear transition to more open farm country and a change in mood. Things feel less cranky and less eccentric south of Portage.

If my many sources were right, there should have been a focus of restless spirits in Portage. The flow of the Wisconsin River, the traditional link to the Fox River system, and history of old Fort Winnebago should have seen to that. But years of inquiry brought no leads.

As often happens with searches, I found this story just as I was about to give up looking. The lead came on an indirect route: a call for assistance in gaining access to traditional spiritual counseling for an American Indian incarcerated at Columbia Correctional Institution.

It was not the first time I had been asked to use my connections to deal with the cultural misunderstandings and paranoia that arise in correctional settings. But it did take a strange turn as my simple desire to help someone find his way through the bureaucratic maze evolved into my last northwoods ghost story.

Wilson was not sure where to start. Despite his range of experience and sophistication, he was frustrated by things seen and heard inside the prison. He asked me to meet him in a room that he had rented in a boarding house near the Soo Line railyard. I was surprised to find it was the very room I had lived in when I worked for the Milwaukee

Road some twenty years earlier. It turned out that our lives overlapped in a number of places.

❦ ❦ ❦

A-ho, ghost hunter! Thanks for coming. The Great Spirit has favored me with the spiritual road and the opportunity to help others. But sometimes the things of the white man confuse me enough that I must ask questions. So we are all teachers and students in our turns.

It is our time to teach each other and for our paths to run together for a time. It is more the surprise that it has not happened before. You know, we are with the same union? Also, do you know that we belong to the same ancient fraternal order? And that we served in the same unit in Vietnam—I was there a year before you—and that we have a mutual friend at the Highground?

We are both open to many possibilities and we both listen to what people have to say. I'm trained as a clinical social worker, but I'm also trained in a number of branches of the Red Road. I'm a Mandan corn priest, by training and part blood. I'm versed in the methods of the Iroquois Society of False Faces. I have studied the traditions of the Delaware holy man, Neolin. I'm an initiated messenger of Gaiwiio, the Seneca good word tradition. I know the sun dance, the peyote ceremony, and the Midewin lodge.

But it is white ways that baffle me. I don't understand chambers of commerce, Jehovah's Witnesses, and demolition derbies. To call attention to one's failings and annoy others, that is a strange thing. What is there about this white medicine that allows or invites public humiliation?

So I must admit it. The spirits here just don't act in ways I understand. Some are petty and whining. Others are dangerous and unpredictable. When we do the sweat lodge on the prison grounds, I can sense dozens of these spirits lurking outside. The power of the lodge, of course, keeps out things that would do harm.

It is inside the prison where the greatest danger lurks. Right in the large room where we do the pipe and drum ceremonies. The Protestants, Catholics, and Muslims use it other times. It's a sterile room, cream-colored concrete block walls, and off-red doors. It's a typical prison space, but somehow even more soulless.

Much of my work has to do with Indian inmates who are being haunted. My first task is to get them to see that these ghosts are not

170

part of the punishment process. Most deserve some form of punishment and a few might even deserve to be haunted. But none deserves the random, psychosis-inducing turmoil that's going on in there. It's cruel and unusual punishment. When I convince them that it's not part of their sentence, then I can work on a medicine strategy to protect them.

That's the frustrating part. I had to study white people's European stories to understand this problem. I couldn't find relevant sacred stories. The closest thing I could find to a road map was that book, *Wisconsin Death Trip*. It's a bit disjointed, being mostly old excerpts from the *Badger State Banner* of Black River Falls.

How can I describe it? It's a catalog of madness from poverty and allegations of hauntings and demonic possession. It's a chronicle of strange suicides by hanging, poisoning, and throat-slashing. It's a compilation of bizarre case studies. Things like insanity from "religious excitement." Things like prim and proper women overtaken by sudden urges to send obscene letters or travel the state breaking windows. Rashes of things like people unconnected to each other and living in different locations deciding to throw themselves in front of trains.

What did I learn? Well, on the most superficial level I found that these things run in waves and cycles. Look back at the 1890s, the 1920s, and the 1950s. And we're sure in one now. I learned that instructions from demons to kill babies were often linked to families with a background of incest. I determined that hermits who died of starvation with food nearby did so because they were too scared to eat.

On the deeper level those old Wisconsin stories helped me gain insight into what's going on within these prison walls. There's the pathology of the place and the supernatural aura of the place. That's partly a function of who they lock up here and what forces the prisoners bring with them. Every prison and jail has some of this baggage. But Columbia is the most loaded I've seen.

These prisons are ideal places for spirits to feed off unfortunate souls. So maybe we are saving ourselves from many problems by drawing those spirits here. Maybe it is this place that is drawing the spirits down the river? Maybe we can bottle them up here?

When we go into the prison sweat lodge we ask these questions. We ask why half the inmates hear voices and what those voices mean. We ask which spirit Dahmer's killer was talking to, which spirits Dahmer left behind, and whether his spirit is still out at Columbia.

In the lodge, we learn more about the tensions between the guards and the administration. It's because the administration has a secret and a secret agenda. They not only know what's going on here, they're experimenting with it.

Usually, if you have people hearing voices you're dealing with multiple personality disorder. Usually a psychiatrist would use hypnosis to contact those other personalities. From a clinical standpoint, hearing voices is a biochemical construct. It always results in a psychiatric diagnosis. In other words, science does not allow for any explained category of hearing voices. It doesn't concede any supernatural explanation. But this way of thinking doesn't square with all the voices at Columbia.

In the lodge we've learned that the voices are manipulated. We have one decent ghost that comes into the lodge and explains what is going on. He's a Menominee from the time of the Black Hawk War. He was a scout for the U.S. Army at Fort Winnebago. He was part of a group that refused to aid in the slaughter of the Sac and Fox people. He and his friends were disposed of and buried in hidden graves right where Columbia was built.

This Menominee ghost is telling us that someone in the administration is linked to these voices. There's a tie to a whole group of professionals high up in state government and the corporations. It's a whole secret cult, devil worship, ritual murders, nude ceremonies, and everything.

The ghost was a victim of distant government treachery and he sees the same pattern in what's going on at Columbia. So there's a thirst for justice here. He wants to break the cycle of evil and of broken promises.

I don't fully understand everything he is teaching us. It's something about a connection between evil, money, corruption, abuse of the earth, and broken promises. It's something that goes back to the beginning of the state. Something that's all bundled up in over a hundred and fifty years of logging, mining, land swindles, and abuse of the living and the dead.

I'm not much of an ecologist. I can't tell you why frogs are being born without all their legs. But the Menominee ghost has helped me understand why all the spirits are stirring. It is the modern way of life that is stirring them up.

Wisconsin has a law prohibiting the disturbance of burial sites. That law is broken all the time. A little payoff here and there, some contractors and politicians who look the other way, and presto, those old bones can be just part of the fill under a highway or a prison. That's what happened with the Menominee ghost. He was dug up, activated, and imprisoned to boot. He can't be put to rest again until he gets some payback.

But he taught me there's a much bigger problem here. It's the pace at which we're disturbing the land. Even though there are ceremonial ways to gain forgiveness for disturbing graves and ways to put most spirits at peace, the sheer amount of building and sprawl creates an incredible number of problems. The burial site protection law is geared around the European notion of a cemetery with a fence around it. But humans have been here for ten thousand years. The whole state—the whole of North America—is a burial site. This means that almost every inch is sacred and needs to be treated as such.

Does that mean that we can't live here? No, we just need to slow down. We need to ask the spirits of all our ancestors how best to proceed. This is hard work, almost like the work of long-term therapy. So, we can't expect quick answers. But we need to get on the spirits' timetable and not the timetable of banks, contractors, and bureaucrats.

The Menominee ghost tells us it is the same today as it was in his day. This hurrying of things faster than the earth can handle always comes down to greed for money and power. That is always the opening for evil.

This kind of evil must always tame the wild things and places to get control. It must tame—or crush—those pockets of independent people outside the mainstream economy and culture. That's the entire goal of the banks, the universities, and the big corporations. Their hirelings from the governors down to the local extension agents work off this agenda. They police the resource colony we call Wisconsin.

The inmates are directly related to this process. The prisons are filled with people who have been disconnected from the land. Some whose ancestors were stolen from their homelands and enslaved. Some, whose ancestors were starved off their homeland long ago. Others who were pushed off farms only a generation or two ago.

The prisons are part of a control structure. And, in the case of Columbia, part of the experiment for further control. But as I said, there's a lot of uncertainty about results. The experiment may run out of control.

The Menominee ghost tells me that spirits are brought here and imprisoned. And he says it is part of a circle. We feed and make strong those imprisoned spirits. They then set in motion the social forces that make us keep building and filling prisons. This will go on in a downward spiral. Unless we can stop this spiral, we will end up breeding a new kind of evil spirit. That will be one that the government won't be able to control. One that will come and go at will.

My part in all this has grown. It started out that I only came to Columbia to offer spiritual comfort and advice. But the Menominee ghost has given me a different job. I have to train warriors here even though my band is made up of spirit-injured men. The task is to find those inmates with that northwoods spirit still in them somewhere.

What will we do with an imprisoned band of warriors? First, we practice the patience and love that will help that Menominee ghost rest and that will reconnect these injured men with Mother Earth. Then we will stand vigil at this place. We will be an outpost for those standing vigil elsewhere. If they are standing vigil to protect the waters, we stand with them. If they stand at a boat landing to protect treaty rights, a potential mine site, to protect our Mother's body, or at a railroad tracks to stop toxic cargo, we will stand with them in spirit.

We will pray, and in doing that, heal these injured men. We will pray and send the power of those prayers to those guarding the earth. Our prayers will send the spirits back up river to where they are needed. Prayer may even get that Menominee ghost back to his people.

My spiritual practice used to be something I kept separate from politics. I never saw much healing in politics. But now I can see that the protection of the sacredness of our land, and the spirits in it, is the political act that we are all called to.